STORE PRESENTATION & DESIGN

STORE PRESENTATION & DESIGN

An International Collection of Design

Martin M. Pegler

VISUAL REFERENCE PUBLICATIONS, Inc., New York, NY

Visual Reference Publications, Inc.
302 Fifth Avenue
New York, NY 10001

Distributors to the trade in the United States and Canada
Watson-Guptill
770 Broadway
New York, NY 10003

Distributors outside the United States and Canada
HarperCollins International
10 E. 53rd Street
New York, NY 10022

Library of Congress Cataloging in Publication Data:
Store Presentation & Design

Printed in China
ISBN 1-58471-035-7

Book Design: Judy Shepard

CONTENTS

INTRODUCTION

I once heard the retail store compared to the tip of an iceberg. It is only that small part of the iceberg visible above the waterline that distinguishes it, but the iceberg is kept afloat by the mass below the waterline. For its success, retail operation depends upon the unseen mass consisting of business acumen, taste, ability to select merchandise, its policies and services. However, the store is judged by the shoppers by the part they see: the store's design, the visual merchandising and the display. That is the tip of the retail iceberg and that is what I call the Trinity of Retail Design. That is what Store Presentation and Design is all about.

Visual Merchandising is a term that came into use only thirty or so years ago. It was meant to replace the term "display" which was by then out of favor with retailers and the people who practiced the craft of "display." Display was considered frivolous, flighty and unnecessary while "visual merchandising" sounded so much more business-oriented and practical. What it should have been called then and should be referred to now is Visual Presentation. Visual merchandising literally mean to "show to sell" but that is also done with magazine and newspaper ads and TV commercials. Products are shown to be sold! Visual Presentation is more than just showing: it is showing product at its best and in the very best way. That means the right setting, the right lighting, the right layout for easy viewing; selecting, assembling and coordinating with accessories; plus the right examples or displays showing how the product can be used or should look.

We have divided this multi-national collection of stores into specific classifications. In the completed stores we show you the "tip of the iceberg": what the shopper sees when all the elements of presentation are put together with taste, talent and with the targeted customer in mind. The stores run the gamut from department, specialty and accessory stores to home furnishing and hard goods store.

No matter what the product—it still requires presentation: good layout, lighting and colors, good fixturing and fittings on which to show the merchandise, and attractive displays to add a sense of excitement and fun to the setting. In a separate cluster we have store fixtures and systems and finally a selection of window displays. The window or up-front presentation of merchandise is the store's "calling card": the first and most important impression maker. It presents not only merchandise coordinated and accessorized and in lifestyle settings but the store's fashion sense or fashion image. The up-front display helps to distinguish the retail store from the others around it.

The buzz word here is PRESENTATION: it is all about the theater in retail design where each day the curtain goes up on a new, different and enticing show of product. Without the lights, the color, sound, smell—and the sense of taste that is defined and enhanced by the visual presentation and display—it is the same ho-hum shopping experience. Presentation makes the difference between whether the store is serving up "comedy" or "tragedy" and how the show will be judged by the shoppers.

So, enjoy this worldwide tour of retail stores across the USA, up to Canada, down to Chile and Brazil and across to England, The Netherlands and Germany—and even to far-off and exotic Japan, South Korea, The Philippines and New Zealand. Behold—no matter what the native culture or language is, PRESENTATION is the universal expression in Retail.

Martin M. Pegler
Author/Editor

STORE PRESENTATION & DESIGN

LA MAISON SIMONS

Carrefour Laval S/C, Laval, QC, Canada

DESIGN: **WATT IDG /Watt International,** Toronto, ON, Canada
SR. DIRECTORS, CREATIVE: **Donna Lawson, Andrew Gallici**
DESIGN TEAM: **Paulis Askevicius, Brian Bettencourt, Merril Fung, Ian Graham, James Nixon, Christian Dinut, Thad Gracz, Joe Wydjaja, Clayton Budd, Carla Conte**
ARCHITECT: **Lemay Michaud, Architecture & Design,** Quebec City, QC
LIGHTING DESIGNER: **LightBrigade Architectural Lighting,** Toronto, ON
PHOTOGRAPHY: **Richard Johnson, Interior Images,** Toronto, ON

This new La Maison Simons—the eighth in the chain of fashion department stores in Quebec—was designed by Watt IDG, a division of Watt International of Toronto. Anchoring the Carrefour Laval shopping center in Laval, just outside of Quebec City, is the 79,000 sq.ft. store with 70,000 sq.ft. on the main level and 9,000 sq. ft. on the mezzanine. The objective set out for the designers was to further the company's brand image, its reputation as a fashion authority and to create a complete "customer experience" which will bring shoppers back again and again. For La Maison Simon it is always important "to maintain a balance between 'old world attention to people' and the avante garde."

For the designers the solution was a store with a modern, streamlined architectural look—"exceptional and unique but not monumental or pretentious," and it had to enhance the Simon's brand experience. The design called for "the space as experience, real entertainment not just cosmetic, an enjoyable and compelling space in which to simply be in, and to explore." That "experi-

ence" begins out front where an internally illuminated glass wall and intersecting canopy "creates a beacon" at each of the exterior entrances. Since the LED lighting is controlled by a program, there is the capability of endless color changes and different looks for the entrances. The massive gridded lattice structures that wrap around the corners of the building will in time be covered with ivy and other foliage. Elongated display windows are modulated into small stories and project them from the facade.

There are strong north/south and east/west aisles that encourage penetration throughout the main level of the store to the hub—women's accessories. Low merchandising walls are topped with illuminated glass display platforms reinforced by dramatic floating walls dropped from the 25 ft. ceiling. "Carefully planned sightlines and the highly visible positioning of the escalators,

perpendicular to the main aisle, ensure traffic penetration to the mezzanine where the linen department is housed."

The architecture of the store creates "appropriate environments" for the different merchandise classifications and the shoppers for that type of merchandiser. Physical spaces ranging from 9 ft. to 37 ft. high are used to differentiate zones and departments—"creating grand spaces with dynamic vistas as well as more intimate and comfortable spaces." The walls are used to break areas and further separate "shopping experiences" as well as optimize merchandise display opportunities. Because of the ceiling heights, integrated displays are often placed over the merchandise in selected areas.

The wide center aisles are highlighted with runway-inspired display platforms which are further accentuated by the illuminated, sandblasted light boxes hanging from the dropped ceiling

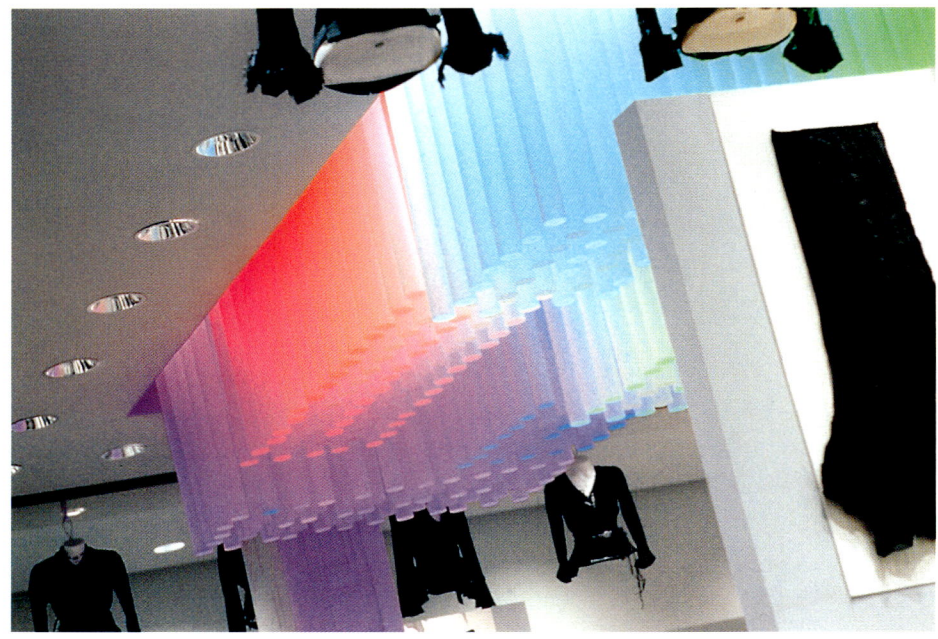

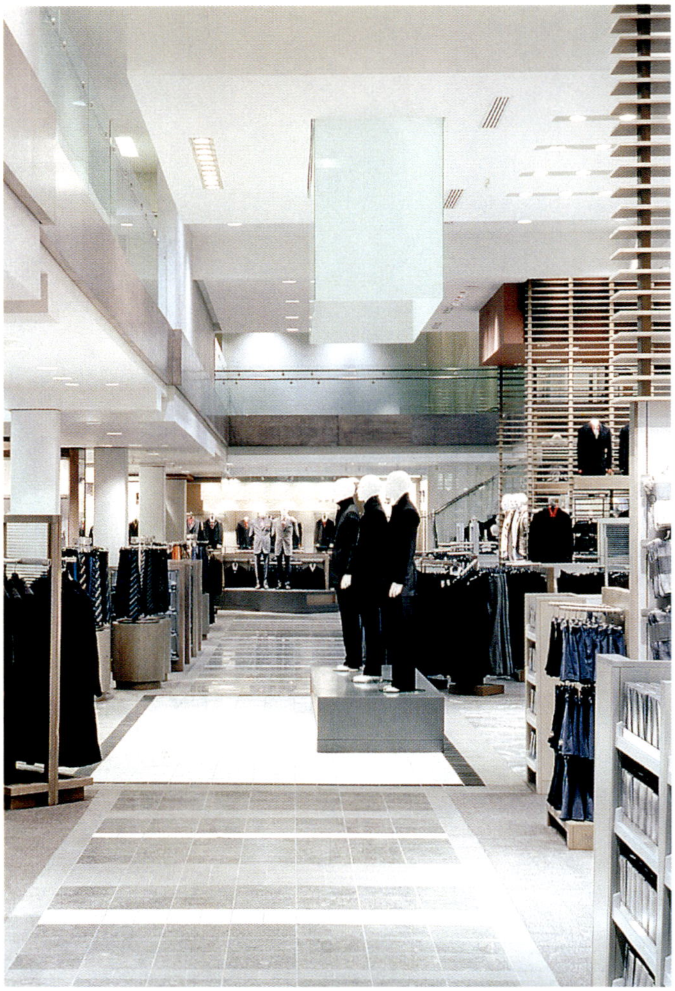

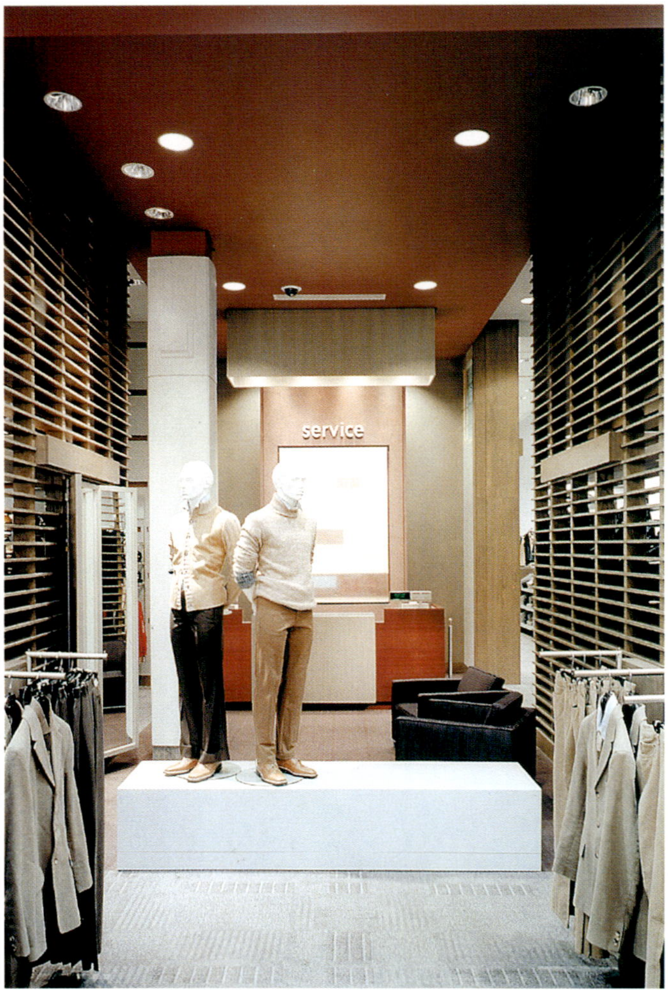
service

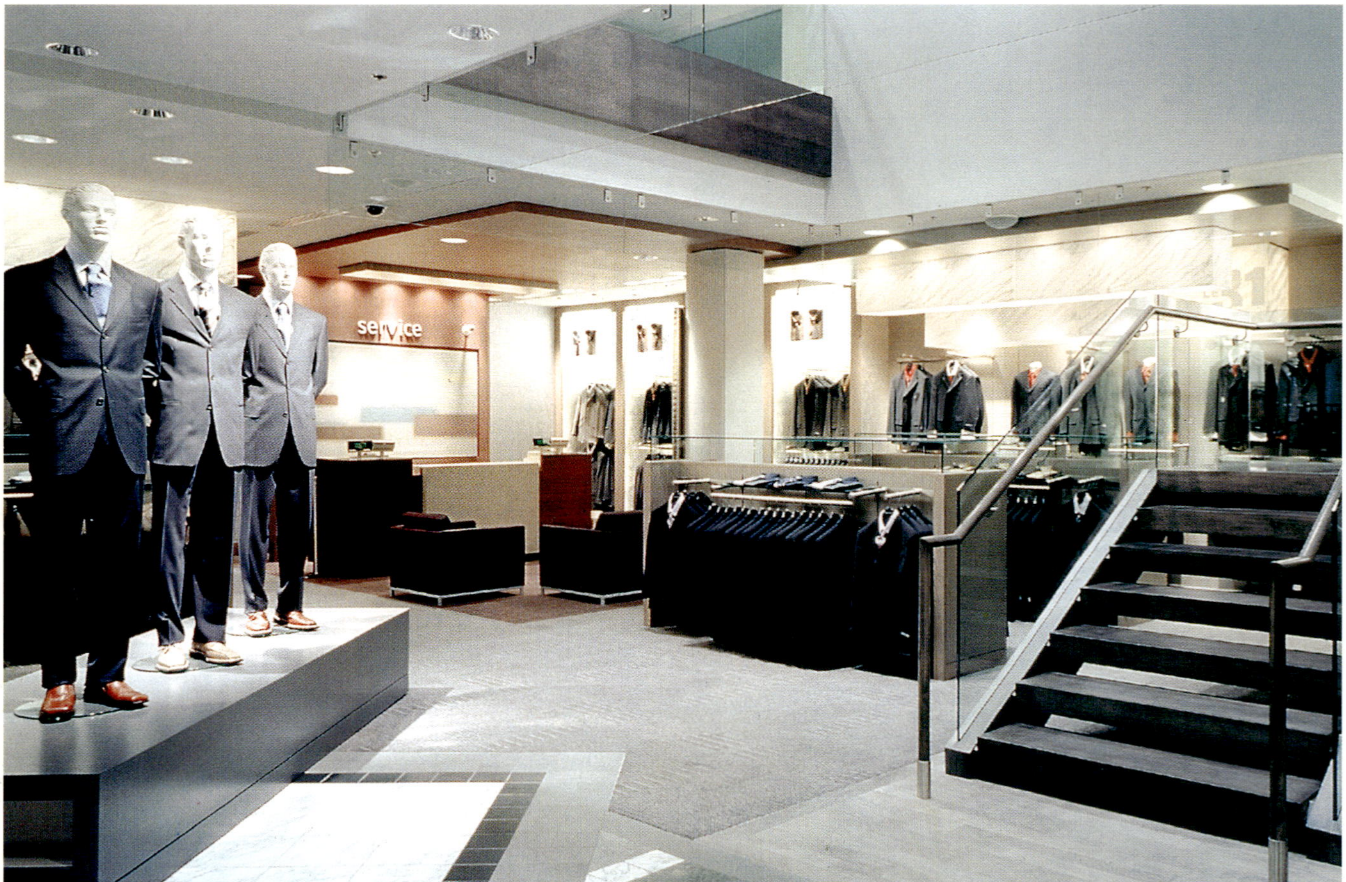
service

blocks above. Throughout, the merchandise displays are designed "to engage the customer in the experience." The custom designed fixtures/fittings are "simple, streamlined and functional" to allow for maximized merchandising and focus on the product. Subtle variations in color, finish and detailing allow each department to express its own, unique identity. In the accessories area the lamps double as mirrors and stools are provided to "encourage the customers to stop, experiment and interact with the product."

The color palette in the store contrasts warm and cool shades and varying tones of gray and white to form "a neutral background allowing the architecture of the space to make a statement without

taking center stage away from the product." Specific color accents are used in some areas or departments and especially to highlight the customer service zones which are so important in enhancing and supporting the perception of high quality service in Simons. Custom carpet and palettes of varying tones and textures of wood, glass, acrylic, vinyl and fabric "combine to create a subtly distinct ambiance for each department."

At Simons the shopping experience is made all encompassing and as comfortable as possible with merchandise always taking center stage. For the fashion conscious and savvy, mid- to up-market teens and adults, La Maison Simon is a home away from home.

NEIMAN MARCUS

Plano, TX

The 150,000 sq. ft. Neiman Marcus store recently opened as an anchor of The Shops at Willow Bend in Plano, TX. The designer, Charles Sparks + Company of Westchester, IL, worked closely with the clients "to introduce an updated format and store design" which the designers describe as "comfortably modern." Together with the client's store planning, facilities planning, visual presentation and lighting consultants, they "combined the disciplines of architecture, interior design, fixture design and lighting design to promote the core concept of the store: Neiman Marcus' commitment to luxury and quality." They attempted to reinvigorate the sense of bold contemporary style long associated with this retailer that for almost 100 years has been an innovator of new retail concepts.

The design team took its inspiration from a mixture of modernist design principles such as the broad, planar surfaces of bold contemporary art and blended it with the flowing lines and grid motifs associated with the "Prairie School" architecture of Frank Lloyd Wright. Low screen and translucent walls "create spaces and backgrounds while maintaining the illusion of space." Neutral colors and lush textiles are combined with rich and unique accents of tinted polished plasters, hand fashioned slumped art glass walls, mother-of-pearl countertops, specially created area rugs and

DESIGN: **Charles Sparks & Company,** Westchester, IL
PRINCIPAL: **Charles Sparks**
PROJECT MANAGER: **Donald Stone**
DESIGN DIRECTOR: **David Koe**
COLOR & MATERIALS: **Fred Wiedenbeck**
PHOTOGRAPHER: **Charlie Mayer,** Chicago, IL

Murano glass light fixtures. The furniture and fixturing are an eclectic mix of contemporary designs and they add detailing and specific personalities to the areas in which they appear. There is a distinct coordination with the design elements of the highly individualized boutiques of such noted designers as Dolce Gabbana, Yves St. Laurent, Armkani, Gucci, Prada, Escada, etc. In addition, there are luxurious fitting rooms located throughout the store which are designed for "speed, comfort and convenience." There is also "an emphasis on detailed amenities such as are found in the finer residences." The first installation of a custom concept for the presentation of Home Decor, China, Crystal, Silver and Tableware appear in this Neiman Marcus in the Gift Gallery. The merchandise is shown in coordinated, individualized room settings.

Other highlights in this NM is the Mariposa Café—a top floor gourmet restaurant—as well as a first floor NM Café. There is also a handsome personal shopper salon which has a very intimate and secluded feeling. For the men there is a VIP area in the Men's Store and throughout the department store the Neiman Marcus collection of fine art is integrated into the interior design of the store.

SELFRIDGES

Exchange Pl., Manchester, UK

PHOTOGRAPHY: **Courtesy of Dula Werke,** Dortmund, Germany

"We wanted to create a Selfridges specifically for Central Manchester providing customers with fresh ideas, entertainment, and even a new lifestyle. We have achieved this by creating a contemporary shopping space with a separate identity and attitude on each floor and by filling it with metropolitan brands to match the needs of the city shopper. In town it is all about immediacy—so the whole store was designed as an immediate experience," said Vittorio Radice, Chief Executive of Selfridges. To make this happen, each of the five floors of the new Selfridges 120,000 sq. ft. store in Exchange Pl. in Manchester was designed by a noted architect/designer including Stanton Williams, Cibic & Partners, David Adjaye, Future Systems and Vincent Van Duysen. All together they created this unique and modern "forum for fashion, food, accessories, music and technology."

The lower ground floor was designed by Future Systems and it is filled with fluid forms and curves that add a stylish quality to the marketplace. Here the shopper finds assorted eateries, gourmet food selections, fresh fruits and vegetables as well as freshly baked breads. The market provides anything from everyday basic needs to the spices and ingredients required for Thai or Asian cuisine. With its sleek, curved walls and units, the almost all-white color scheme is interspersed with splashes of strong colors and cool blue flooring.

The ground or main level houses accessories and beauty areas. Designed by the "modernist designer," David Adjaye, the airy and contemporary space is filled with displays of the major cosmetic and toiletry brands. "The idea was to create an airy and vibrant space that shows off the fantastic brands on offer and to create a

place which encourages customers to be both playful and indulgent," said the designer, David Adjaye. Of special interest here is the illuminated Perspex ceiling which is designed to radiate light. Another focal element is the dynamic main atrium which affords visitors a wonderful view of the cantilevered second floor restaurant designed by Stanton Williams who also designed the women's second floor. From the atrium it is possible to get glimpses of the floors above and below, and the stunning glass staircase that connects the levels.

Black stained timbers and gray resin flooring cover the formalwear and designer denim sections of the first floor which was created by Vincent Van Duysen in his fashionable minimalist style. Stainless steel, nickel and white glass complete the neutral palette. He varies the color scheme "to signal the change in brands" and thus, in Men's Spirit and contemporary areas the walls and resin floors are "dirty" yellow. The Lab area is all white in contrast. In this "temple

of cutting-edge cool" shoppers will find such noteworthy labels as Alexander McQueen, Versace, Dolce & Gabbana and Evisu.

To affect a more intimate feeling on the second floor where the women's fashion are on display, Stanton Williams sectioned off areas of the floor with varied floor treatments featuring resin and stone. "With so many cutting-edge designer brands in one space we decided to create a stage or exhibition area allowing customers to see a multitude of brands at a glance," commented Stanton Williams.

The Italian design firm, Cibic & Partners, were entrusted with the third floor which contrast sharply with what went before and is more "playful" in concept and style. Here the space is dominated by the scarlet resin floor, the curved white walls and the light gray marcarno ceiling blocks. Stainless steel and colored plexiglass add additional sparkle to this floor. These reflect "Selfridges innovative concept of housing entertainment and 'Spirit'

(the store's young and trendy fashions) in the same environment." Dula Werke of Dortmund, Germany—the noted shopfitting designers and manufacturers—were actively involved in the design and production of the fixtures and fittings that add so much to the look of the TV and book sections of this floor—many of the fixtures that are used on the men's level. The illustrations, shown here, refer mainly to the men's level and the third level and the Dula created and executed fixtures and fittings that are so prominently shown.

According to James Bidwell, Marketing Director of Selfridges, "The creative interior design of the store gives customers something new at every turn—through variations on lighting, colors and materials—whilst each floor has an individual identity they still carries the Selfridges design hallmarks of style, innovation and theater." Is this multi-designer use a look for the future of department store design?

HARVEY NICHOLS

Edinburgh, Scotland, UK

DESIGN: **FOUR IV Design Consultants,** London, UK
MANAGING DIRECTOR: **Chris Dewar Dixon**
PHOTOGRAPHY: **Courtesy of FOUR IV**

Some department stores or specialty stores "cookie-cut" little clones of their flagship operations while others—more in tune with the ever-changing times—see each new store as an opportunity to create a newer, fresher and more suitable retail image of itself. Stores such as Saks Fifth Avenue and Neiman Marcus in the U.S. are forever re-inventing themselves as they adapt to new locations. The Harvey Nichols stores in the UK are just as forward thinking.

With this new 90,000 sq. ft. store that opened only months ago in Edinburgh, "The wait is over for the style conscious Scots." FOUR IV, the noted London design consultancy, has come up with a new, cool and contemporary interior with all the "pure Harvey Nichols glamour" intact. Targeted at the "upmarket luxury shoppers," this new five story building anchors the very upscaled new retail development in St. Andrews Square. The designers used a cool palette of limestone, smoked mirror, walnut, chrome and rich black lacquer enhanced with "specialist multi-colored light refractive surfaces to form the perfect backdrop to the brands." The latest in technology was also included in the design but with a "special Harvey Nichols twist." A white-on-white LED strip rises from the ground level through the central atrium to the top floor. Over 35 ft. of brand messages are relayed on the strip. Launches and lunches are only two of the messages and "the visual stimulation continues via large plasma screens playing the latest catwalk shows."

FOUR IV has created a discreet retailing system specifically for this installation. "The system of minimal linear channels in aluminum clearly expresses the values of the

Harvey Nichols brand while providing a flexible, discreet framework for individual brands to sit within." HN has a reputation for exclusive and desirable designer name brands and to provide "theater and anticipation," there are five illuminated glass tanks which look out onto the central atrium. Featured signature pieces of merchandise from each floor "illustrate the breadth of the offer."

"Beyond Beauty"—on the ground level—offers shoppers an "holistic experience for all the senses." Along with skin products there is a juice bar. Other exclusive cosmetic brands are also featured on this level along with jewelry. Within a 12,500 sq. ft. area "menswear" showcases "the best in contemporary, formalwear and casualwear" with brands such as Gucci, Comme des Garcons, Christisan Dior and Marc Jacobs.

The "womenswear" collection fills two floors with "pure fashion housing a mix of international

designers and contemporary collections." Prada, McQueen, Chloe and Dolce & Gabbana are also shown here and there are special departments for lingerie, footwear and children's wear where the clothing is displayed on magnetic wall panels.

"Harvey Nichols is all about fashion, beauty, glamour and impeccable service, so it has been essential to capture these elements and communicate them clearly to the customers through the retail environment," said Chris Dewar Dixon, Managing Director of the design firm. The consultancy has been working with Harvey Nichols for over nine years and FOUR IV is now working on the next full size HN department store scheduled to open in Manchester this year.

LOTTE PUSAN

Pusan, South Korea

DESIGN: **Pavlik Design Group,** Ft. Lauderdale, FL
PRESIDENT/CEO: **R. J. Pavlik**
CREATIVE DIRECTOR: **Sherif Ayad**
SR. PROJECT DESIGNER: **Fernando Castillo**
DESIGN ADMINISTRATION DIRECTOR: **Placido Herrera**
DIRECTOR OF PROJECT: **Armando Castillo**
KOREAN BRANCH MANAGER: **Phillip Hwang**
PHOTOGRAPHY: **Kwang Wook, Kim**

Imagine walking down the Faubourg Ste. Honore in Paris, Madison Ave. in New York City, Bond St. in London or almost any side street in Milan! Imagine finding one exclusive designer boutique standing next to another— all facing the same street! Well, the fashionable, upscale shoppers in Pusan, South Korea do not have to go to any of these far off places or take any chances about changes in the weather now that all of this is available to them in the newly opened Imported Boutiques Collection in the Lotte Department store.

Lotte wanted the Pavlik Design Team to create "an exclusive upscale fashion galleria in a luxurious design that complemented the expanded haute couture shops and their fashions." What Lotte did get is evidenced in these views; it is a specialty arcade of the world's finest designer shops in the Pusan flagship store. Pusan is on the east coast of Korea and is a relatively large city with an affluent society. The store in part of a larger complex. Occupying 22,500 sq. ft., it is a "street of shops" with plazas, atriums, and grand staircases that create a multi-level fashion esplanade. Though basically laid out on two major levels there are mezzanines between them that add to the dramatic movement within this space. Though each of the individual boutiques was designed by the particular vendor, the objective for Pavlik's team was to create a framework that carried forth the Lotte image while an assortment of retail environments—each with its unique design agenda—would fit into that overall ambiance. The neutral, understated, "floating facades" created a contemporary classic framework "that allowed an otherwise generic collection of shops to now become distinctive with its new luxurious Lotte sig-

nature." Grand open approaches with soft, curving ramps "creating formal arrival points" to the European-style "Boulevard of Fashion." Curving walls with asymmetrical light coves add variety and softness to "potentially straight, narrow circulation." The spaces are unified by the sleek, back-lit white frames which also contain the diverse designs and materials of the individual boutique shop fronts. It is as though each shop has two facades: the generic, back-lit white marble frame of the overall Lotte design into which is recessed the designer's own entrance design.

Polished black granite floors swirling with asymmetrical patterns and insets of white marble not only complement the "street" concept but highlight and accentuate the "arrival points" previously mentioned. According to the designers, "Obstructive structural and mechanical elements created design challenges that have been transformed into floating backdrops, sparkling stages and fashion vignettes that are strategically featured throughout the space." In addition, adding to the drama of the design concept, is the lighting; the back-lit facades and the floating ceiling planes throughout.

At a time when department stores are attempting to reclaim their place in the retail scene, it is important that the department store itself—as a brand image—become uppermost in the shopper's mind and not the many vendor shops that seem to inhabit the store. This is an excellent example of how the retailer—Lotte—has taken control of an expanse of vendor shops/designer boutique and created its own unique brand look that dominates the space yet allows each vendor to still have control of its own area or shop.

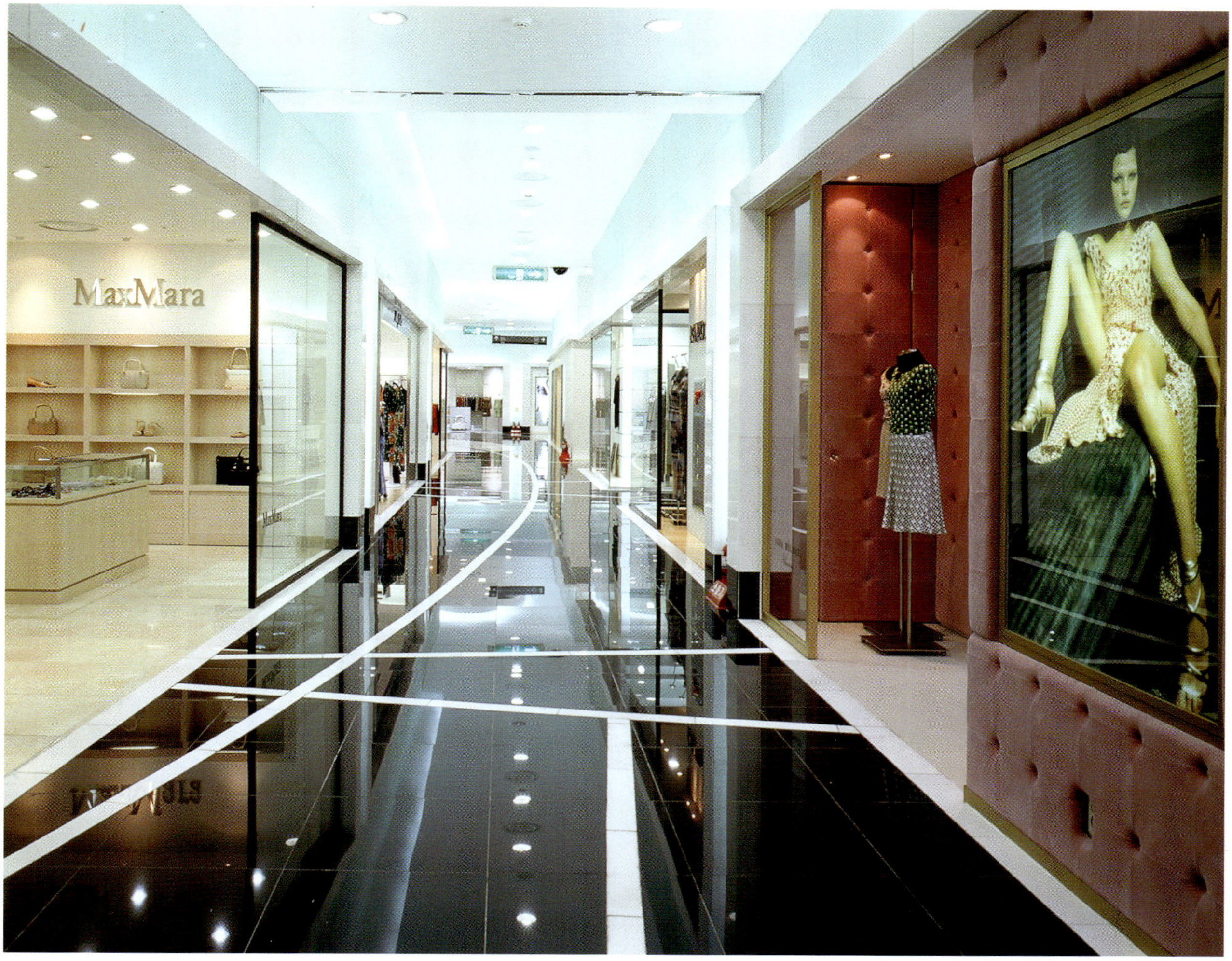
MaxMara

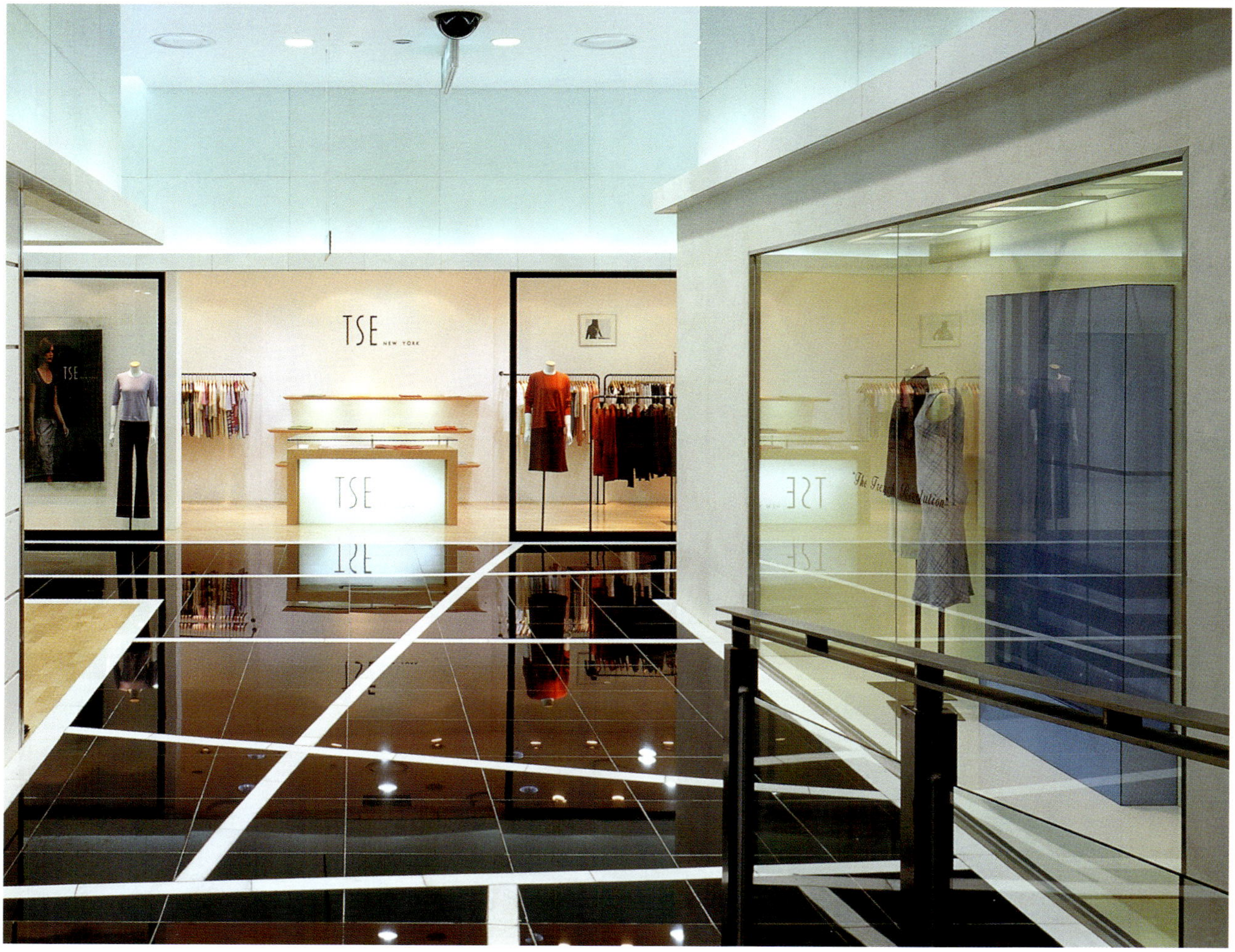
TSE
NEW YORK
TSE

RIPLEY

The Pavlik Design Team of Ft. Lauderdale was called upon by Ripley, an outstanding department store chain located mainly in Chile, to remodel the existing store located in the upscale Parque Arauco shopping center. This major shopping center is located on the outskirts of Santiago and thus draws shoppers from in-town as well as the surrounding affluent suburbs. The design directive from the Ripley management was simple—"Establish Ripley as a contemporary fashion destination," and, as always today, the underlying factor was to attract the younger shoppers to this store.

Though Ripley already has a very strong brand image, it is primarily with the older demographic groups. The malls, however, are more and more filling up with exciting, colorful and youth-oriented specialty stores where the younger shoppers flock. To counteract that flow and introduce Ripley to this fashion-forward seeking clientele, Pavlik's designers—who already have created the very successful "youth-bridge" with their Litio design for El Palacio de Hierro stores in Mexico—created this new look filled with "fresh contemporary theaters of fashion."

The designers installed "unique fashion zones" within the light, bright and airy space. The "shops" are defined by the special floor and ceiling elements and the back-lighted glass columns. Together they help reinforce the main traffic patterns within the store. These "paths" are accentuated by the illuminated glass floor walkways. To either side are "floating fixtures and wall slabs" that help to distinguish each shop while affecting what is perceived as "a street of shops." On the main level, in the cosmetics area, the curving glass floor walkway snakes its way past the coolly illuminated columns that support the cut-out and patterned ceiling.

DESIGN: **Pavlik Design Team,** Ft. Lauderdale, FL
PRESIDENT/CEO: **R.J. Pavlik**
VP: **Luis Martin**
DESIGN DIRECTOR: **Luis Valladares**
DESIGN ADMINISTRATIVE DIRECTOR: **Placido Herrera**
ASST. PROJECT DIRECTOR: **Christy Morales**
PROJECT MANAGERS: **Manuel Codero, Connie Kehren**
LIGHTING DESIGNER: **Amy Ann Straley**

PHOTOGRAPHY: **Guy St. Clair Photography,** Nunoa, Santiago, Chile

The almost all-white ambiance enhances the light and airy feeling of this floor.

Throughout this sleek, clean, modern interior bold color accents are used to highlight or demarcate particular areas or shops. The floors are mostly white tile but in some departments it is patterned or bordered with vivid blue tiles. Feature walls pop out from the overall white environment in rich, earthy reds, ocher yellows and deep blues. In keeping with the "now" look and the "youth oriented" approach, giant graphics of the targeted market are integrated with the architecture. In some instances they are used as "signage" as well as decor or to highlight "dramatic arrival points and focal shops."

All through this dramatically illuminated space there are high impact visuals and statements that reach out to create a new and exciting look for this established department store operation.

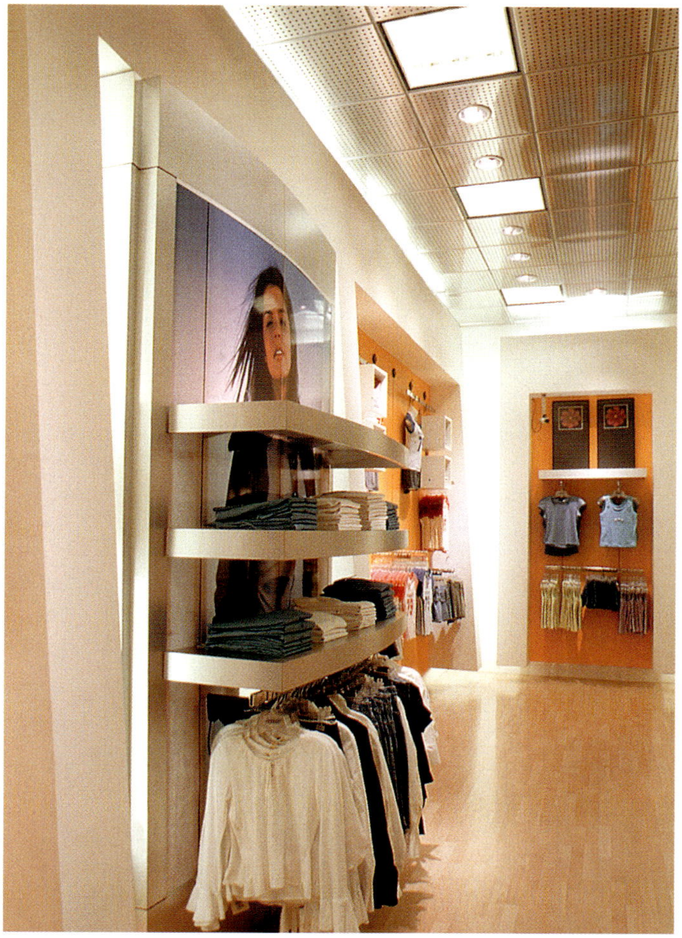

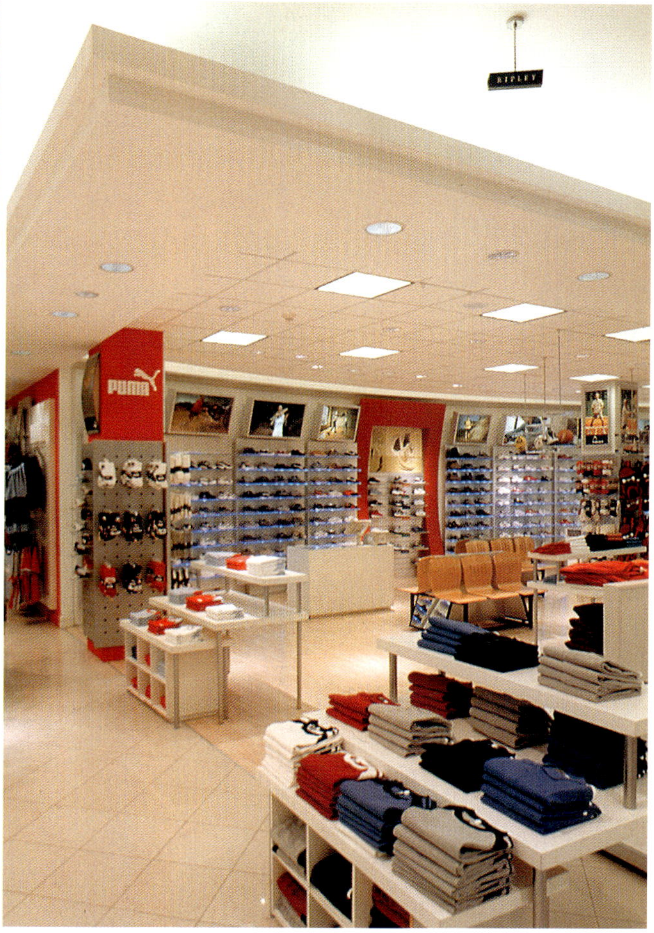
PUMA

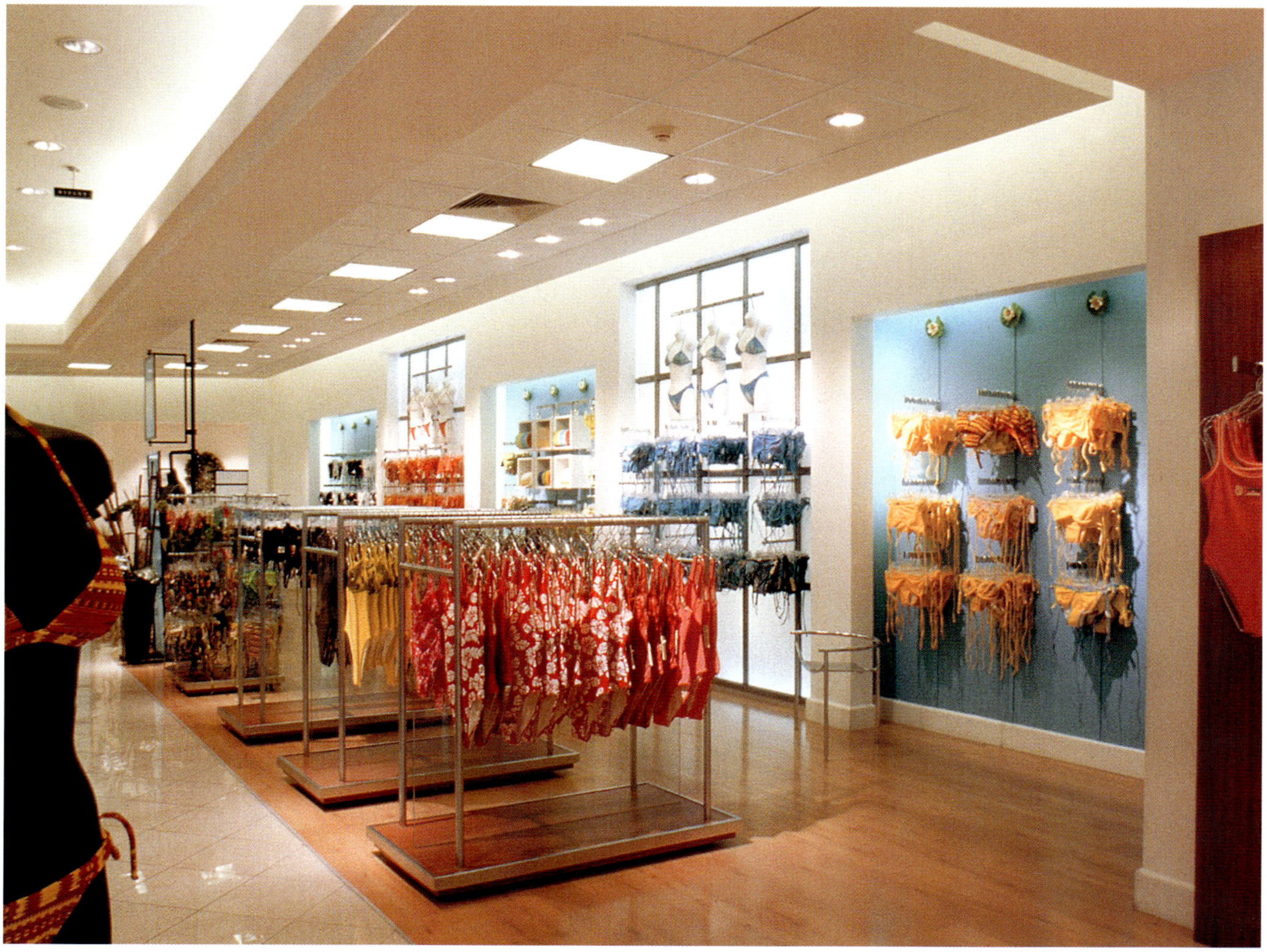

CHRISTIAN LACROIX

Daikanyama, Shibuya-Ku, Tokyo, Japan

The new Christian Lacroix 2,600 sq. ft. shop in the Shibuya-Ku district of Tokyo is the result of a one year collaboration between Christian Lacroix, the noted fashion designer, and Christophe Carpente—the architect-conceptor and the principal of CAPS Architects of Zurich. The statement by Christian Lacroix that follows best sums up this new retail concept for the very avant garde designer.

"I wanted to go beyond the usual simple white cube to re-establish the balance between 'geometric' and 'organic.' I also wanted to respect all the places where we are likely to recognize ourselves as well as strongly ensuring our presence and our identity, yet without negating the existing framework or architecture and by giving the sensation that, like all circus

or fair grounds, we might fly away from one day to the next like all 'travelers' do. 'Travel' in the widest sense has always been a constant in my work and, if I had to choose a word that resumes this taste, it would be 'nomad' or 'nomadism'; therefore, with Christophe Carpente, we have dreamed up an almost retractile, mobile device, adapted according to necessities and to instituted places. A contemporary caravanserai of multi-color glass structures, transparently creating for the eyes that look through them, the perspective of an infinite variety of 'rainbow' tones.

The indispensable technical or computer elements will be concealed in an apparent pile of variegated metallic boxes, like a child's building set. The rectilinear architecture of

DESIGN: **CAPS Architects,** Zurich, Switzerland
DESIGN TEAM: **Sabine Henning, Elizabeth Lockard, Marc Perrin, Tomas Zenker**
LOCAL ARCHITECT: **Axe Design LTD.,** Tokyo, **Toshio Sano**
ARTWORK: **Bernard Quesnaiux**
PHOTOGRAPHY: **Nacasa & Partners**

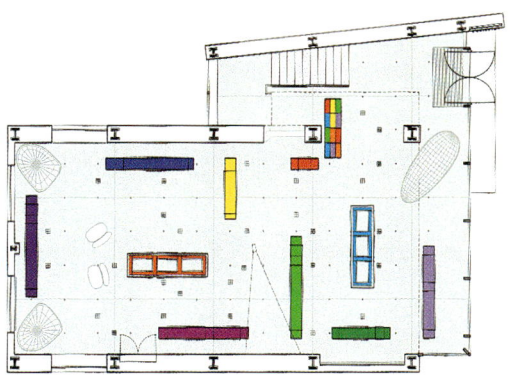

GROUND FLOOR

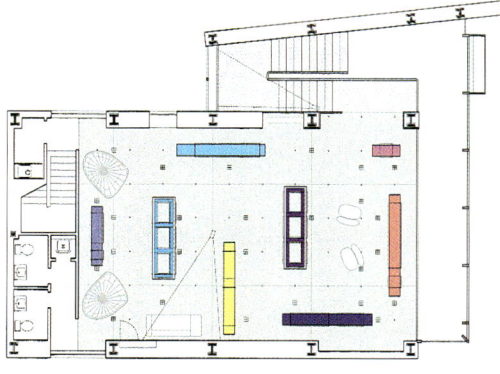

MEZZANINE

37

the mobiles set in brushed metal is softened by the curves of some seats signed by Pierre Paulin, that are upholstered in bright tone-on-tone wools. The abstraction of all these chromatic volumes contrast with the botanical elements, 'lobster pot/console,' and 'cabin/tent' in 'rhatan,' elaborated like enormous wickerwork baskets—or with the eccentric—a wink at velvet or quilted satin, a few touches of golden wood or silver canvas. The walls remain pure, naked, in a slightly pearly virginal white, animated by poetic, dynamic and playful video images or punctuated with photos and paintings by artist friends such as Joel Bartolomo, Delphine Kreuter, Nils Udo and Bernard Quesniaux, whose

works often nourish mine and thus participate in a movement where one day we must all reunite."

Thus, the peripheral whitened walls serve to support "artistic inventions" and the ceiling is designed like a regular screen independent from the floor. The lighting is direct to accent the products exclusively and on to the walls which, according to the CAPS team, "accordingly reveals the colors of the furnishings in transparency." The floor is a flagstone of smooth cement indexed by polished steel anchoring points for furniture and also by steel sections.

The plan is organized "like a labrynth—structured by colored glass pebbles supporting the products and gathered around a collection theme."

Only the furnishings articulate the traffic pattern which is varied by "contrasting organic shapes (tables, counters, fitting rooms, seating and cash desks)." No window display blocks the view into the shop—"leaving a maximum amount of transparency." The facade surface carries a hand written text by Christian Lacroix that is printed from top to bottom of the ten meter (32') facade "in see-through material and reflecting an iridescent diffraction of light."

MULBERRY

Bond St., London, UK

DESIGN: **FOUR IV,** London, UK

A new experience awaited the "luxury shopper" when Mulberry—"the quintessentially English brand" store for men's and women's fashions—opened its bronze "garden gates" to the newly refurbished flagship store on Bond St. The retail designer and branding specialist, FOUR IV, of London, created this dramatic metamorphosis which was geared to put Mulberry on the map for a new customer base "with a complete kit of creative ideas that will detail every stitch of the Mulberry Experience across the world." Mulberry is looking to attract the "thirty-something" affluent shopper with this new look.

FOUR IV researched the market to find out what Mulberry represented in that luxury brand area of shopping. "This highlighted where

Mulberry could best capitalize on its unique origins and inherent brand idiosyncrasies." Based on the results —"English"—"inspirational"—"aspirational"—the designers used these concepts to communicate the brand through the store design, the product presentation and the graphics. The distinctive Mulberry tree was retained as the brand logo but redrawn "to bring it in line with the new modern luxury values of the company."

By combining the twin ingredients of fine leather and fastidious detailing, the designers were able to fulfill the design brief generated by the research. Mulberry was founded by Roger Saul as a venue for selling the fine belts and bags he designed and as FOUR IV saw it—the "essence" of Mulberry is "part Saul quirky genius and part

English witty chic." The new store design exudes this character and the re-evaluated brand's focused and coherent ranges of leather accessories, contemporary clothing and home goods are given individual areas in the store. Menswear is on the lower ground level and features a leather clad rear wall with "secret panels" that open into the changing rooms. It is all quite reminiscent of old, stately homes. Patterns of the landscaped formal gardens at the Mulberry plant were carved into the rug on the floor and a long table—"an iconic piece for the new Mulberry"—is made of oak and inset with leather. Throughout, English craftspersons were commissioned to create "unique structures focusing on the essence and techniques deployed by Mulberry." There

are custom-designed leather man-nequins and bronze and timber rails hanging on leather straps as well as clothes-horse type frames which carry men's trousers much as the uncut leathers would be supported on the factory floor.

Leather accessories, luggage and home goods—each in its own unique environment—cohabit on the ground level where chocolate-colored lime-stone is laid in the various settings. A leather paneled staircase leads up past the conservatory and the custom porcelain chandeliers to the Great Hall above. Here, a huge beveled mir-ror reflects down the length of the signature long oak tables. "Suede walled changing rooms create boudoir lavishness." The leather detailing

which is featured throughout is fin-ished in oxblood—the Mulberry cor-porate color—and tan. The new oxblood is richer and darker in tone and sets off the redrawn Mulberry tree. The tree also "lives" on in the packaging: each is tied with a ribbon onto which a silk Mulberry leaf is affixed and the suit carriers and shoe bags are sealed with leather ties.

According to Chris Dewar Dixon, the Managing Director at FOUR lV, "To develop a new vision for such an iconic English brand has been chal-lenging and rewarding both personal-ly and professionally. Mulberry is not just another luxury brand; it has vision, a real family and it now has a bold and true way of expressing its uniqueness."

JEAN PAUL GAULTIER

Madison Ave., New York, NY

Adding to the ever growing list of luxury boutiques in New York City and on Madison Avenue, is the new 2,750 sq. ft. (260 sq. meters) shop devoted to the stylish fashions and accessories of Jean Paul Gaultier. It is the first Gaultier free-standing boutique in the U.S. In the next five years the company plans to open 20 boutiques internationally and to use this New York boutique concept—as designed by the famous French designer, Philippe Starck, in collaboration with the fashion designer, Jean Paul Gaultier—as its prototype. This will "create the global network of stores that reflect Jean Paul Gaultier's creative vision and showcase his unique designs."

The vision of the design was achieved by combining the brightness of "tadelakt"—a material inspired from North Africa, India and the Middle East—with the transparency of delicate crystal and the reflections of mirrors. Added to this palette is the smoothness of padded taffeta used to create upholstered niches within which the garments are displayed on ornate brass and stainless steel hanging units. The soft walls contrast with the large, engraved multi-colored mirror screen. Tables, dressers and display counters are also finished with engraved mirrors and seem to disappear in the space that is filled with soft, glowing reflections. Adding to the sumptuous quality of the shop are the crystal chandeliers with silk shades that contribute to the sparkling environment while providing a soft ambient glow to the space. Of special note is the giant replica of the signature Gaultier "dressform" perfume bottle that now becomes a statue or idol set upon a mirrored base and surrounded by actual size bottles displayed on the tufted taffeta panels that line the niche.

"The continual movement of images, projected onto the wall at the entrance, completes the fairy tale-like environment. It is a perfect representation of what the Jean Paul Gaultier style stands for."

DESIGN: **Philippe Starck,** Paris, France
in collaboration with Jean Paul Gaultier

LILLIE RUBIN

North Star Mall, San Antonio, TX

DESIGN/ARCHITECT: **Michael Malone Architects,** Dallas, TX
PRINCIPAL IN CHARGE OF DESIGN: **Michael Malone, AIA**
PROJECT MANAGER: **Rob Romero**
PROJECT ARCHITECT: **Talmadge Smith**
PHOTOGRAPHY: **Jud Haggard Photography,** Bellaire, TX

For over 50 years the name Lillie Rubin has been associated with the place sophisticated, upscale women went for special occasion/evening dresses. Recently the chain was taken over by Cache who felt that there was still a market—though aging—for the Lillie Rubin type of merchandise. Michael Malone Architects of Dallas was called upon to create the new prototype for a new, larger market. "The design was to provide a bridge and welcome new customers by being brighter, more open and fun." Also, to appeal to the younger market, without losing the established clientele, management decided to bring in more business attire and sportswear and thus the new design would need to support such a merchandise mix.

The design solution, shown here in the 2,100 sq. ft. space in the North Star Mall in San Antonio, features a more open and inviting facade design with floor-to-ceiling glass that serves as "the window into the store." The design is "classic" so a variety of merchandise can be shown in a setting that is not quickly dated. The desire was to "romance" the client but not with literal visual clues such as marble and crystal chandeliers. The two-toned interior is creme and black. The up front platforms hold classic matching mannequins and simple lifestyle photos. Simple floor fixtures in stainless steel and black show off the featured outfits while the stock is displayed in flexible wall bays on hang bars and face-outs that are supported by the recessed standards in the perimeter walls.

It was important that this new design not "scare off the existing customers" but make them feel comfortable in the new environment. The soft, sweeping line of the cash/wrap, which also serves as the jewelry and fragrance display case, suggests the sensuous lines of a grand piano—"the perfect accessory for any special event." That shape is also picked up and reiterated in the tiered ceiling "clouds" that provide the ambient lighting as it washes across the ceilings. The merchandise and the displays are accented by fixed halogen down lights and the light is reflected off the large, creme colored, porcelain tiles on the floor. "The wall and ceiling color is used throughout the store and was selected, in part, because of its softening glow when reflected onto the skin."

The design was created to be rolled out, easily built and maintained in other locations yet still maintain the Lillie Rubin reputation for service and quality that it has always had.

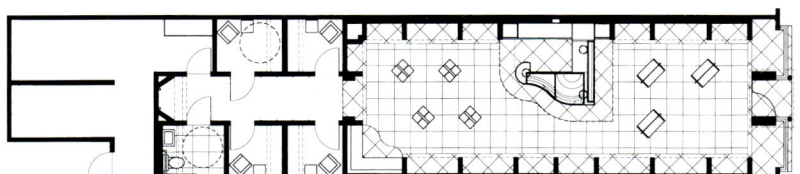

DUNHILL

Ginza, Namiki-Dori, Tokyo, Japan

DESIGN CONCEPT & PROJECT DESIGN:
CAPS Architects, Zurich, Switzerland
CAPS TEAM: **Christophe Carpente, Thomas Madory,**
Richard Kevic, Claudio Tortelli
LOCAL ARCHITECT: **AXE Design Ltd.,** Toshio Sano, Japan
PHOTOGRAPHY: **Nacasa & Partners**

This Tokyo store is almost 2,700 sq. ft. and also has two levels: retail on the entrance level and a lounge area above. The store front is almost all glass accented with copper moldings and "cigar brown render."

A view through the glass into the bright red glow of the interior and the bamboo wood flooring.

The lounge area on the upper level with the loden upholstered sofas.

The retail area with its Mondrian inspired arrangement of shadow boxes lined up against the red walls. Plasma screens fill some of the uppermost boxes. Brown leather edged with white stitching finish the tops of the gray marmorino wood floor fixtures.

SACADA

Rio de Janiero, Brazil

Sacada is a chain of stylish shops featuring elegant and fashionable garments for women in their 30s and 40s. Currently there are ten shops located in upscale malls and on fine shopping streets in Rio de Janiero and they have all been designed by Arthur Matteo de Casas. The stores, according to Casas, have "a contemporary atmosphere and are at the same time sober and light." The result, as shown here, is a dynamic and quite dramatic architectural setting with masses of light and dark combined with the subtle light in a refined, minimal composition.

The rich materials appear understated because of the total neutrality of the palette. Pale beige travertine marble tiles line the floor and the generous block of volume that is the counter/cash-wrap. Complementing the warm color of the marble and the off-white painted walls and ceiling is the Ipe wood—a very dark Brazilian wood—which is used extensively in the design. Its deep color reappears as a veneer on one long wall upon which the barely discernible black dresses are hung on floating stainless steel rods. The same wood also faces some of the cabinetry behind the travertine counter and the two ample tables that go with the off-white leather bolsters and pillows that make up the major seating and dividing area in the center of the shop.

General lighting and some accenting is provided by the directional dicroic spots in the ceiling. Recessed fluorescent lights—directly over the wall hung garments—provides the necessary illumination for the black dresses which seem to be "the specialty of the house."

DESIGN: **Studio Casas, Arthur Matteo de Casas**
PHOTOGRAPHY: **Courtesy of Arthur Casas**

ANTHROPOLOGIE

The Grove, Los Angeles, CA

Anthropologie is not just a store: it is a complete lifestyle—a way of thinking, dressing and furnishing one's personal environment. In many ways Anthropologie was an innovator of lifestyle merchandising when its first retail store opened in a converted auto showroom in Pennsylvania. It presented an unusual mix of apparel with accessories, home furnishings, garden decor and gift items. Then, as now, the store design and the creator of the visual brand setting for this unique type of product offering is Ron Pompei and his staff at Pompei A.D. of New York City. With this new store, at The Grove in Los Angeles, Pompei A.D. has created the 35th special, site-specific Anthropologie store in the U.S. "Central to the concept and values of Anthropologie is the ongoing organic evolution of the richly-textured, high touch store environments."

Located in the historic Farmer's Market in Los Angeles, the store features a wood canopy that extends out over the 24 ft. wide open entrance. The rough timber, an Anthropologie signature material, creates a strong horizontal plane that breaks across the otherwise two-story high glass shop front. Based on the circular, multi-ringed lighting fixtures used in mosques—especially those in Hagia Sophia in Istanbul, the designers have created a massive 25 ft. diameter black, wrought iron chandelier that dominates the cool, vast, stone-like interior. A floor-to-ceiling natural tree trunk rises up to complement the wide swath of rough timber that affects the equally impressive horizontal plane on the entrance wall.

Throughout the space there is an eclectic mix of periods, styles, kinds of furniture and fixtures and dramat-

DESIGN: **Pompei A.D., LLC.,** New York, NY
DESIGN PRINCIPAL: **Ron Pompei**
STUDIO DIRECTOR: **Nicholas Arauz**
DIR. OF PROFESSIONAL PRACTICE: **Tim Bittner**
PROJECT MANAGER: **Gerard Orozco**
PROJECT TEAM: **John Ginnochio, Colin Brice, Scot Campbell, Rayann Shums, Annika Newell**

For Anthropologie:
PRESIDENT: **Glen Senk**
CREATIVE DIRECTOR: **Kristin Norris**
DIRECTOR OF SALES: **Wendy Brown**
DISTRICT MERCHANDISER: **Karen Heilbroner**
DIRECTOR OF CONSTRUCTION: **Ben Weinraub**

PHOTOGRAPHY: **Tom Bonner,** Venice, CA

JILL

Makati, Philippines

The 1,500 sq. ft. Jill store in Makatri, Philippines is a new brand launch for the well known Rusitan Department Stores based in the Philippines. As designed by RPA, it is a "collection-based shop with a succinct look" and the collection is moderate ladies' fashion apparel for work, leisure and sleep. The challenge for the designers was to make sure that the design did not overpower the merchandise nor make it appear too upscale or sophisticated for the targeted market. "We needed to make sure the customer felt special and we were meeting her wardrobe needs."

Instead of focusing on the wall, the designers concentrated on the floor which is designed to resemble a cityscape. "The tall fixtures—representing skyscrapers—are attached at the ceiling and the floor and are bridges meant to encourage exploration throughout the shop thus letting the customer experience and understand the collection." The rear wall mimics a hang bar from the customer's closet and the colored wall soffits direct shoppers to the cash/wrap. Under the soffits, a black wall—with focused merchandise—leads the shoppers into the gray tiled area where the merchandise is "bulked out"—or presented in quantity. The overall environment is neutral and minimal with accents of black and celery green. Colors will change seasonally to reflect the seasonal colors of the clothing.

Graphics play a vital role in the design of the shop and in communicating the brand message. Large graphic images identify each zone within the shop. They are accompanied by taglines: She Works, She Plays, She Dreams. The graphics are important in delineating each "experience" and since the space is wide and shallow—customers have full access to all of the merchandise messages.

The success of this prototype will determine how many and where the future Jill stores will be rolled out.

DESIGN: **Retail Planning Associates (RPA)**
Columbus, OH, www.rpaworldwide.com

RPA Team
PARTNER, INTERNATIONAL SERVICES: **Peter McIlroy**

SR. STUDIO OFFICER: **Nicolas Baughman**
ASSOC. MERCHANDISER/PLANNER: **Jason Woods**
SR. MERCHANDISER/PLANNER: **Marie Haines**
ENVIRONMENTAL DESIGNERS: **Angela Hunhziker
& Paul Steeples**
SR. DOCUMENTATION SPECIALIST: **Johanna Castle**
RETAIL STRATEGIST: **Stephen Jay**
SR. LIGHTING DESIGNER: **Perry Kotick**

For "JILL"
**Bienvenido R. Tantoco, Jr./Ramon Vincente T.
Roxas/Robt. M. Dowley/Michael V. Gonzalez/
Girlie Msarie V. Alamag/Vida T. Estrella**
GRAPHICS: **J. Walters,** Manila

LEVI'S

Berlin, Germany

It was not an easy design challenge. Checkland Kindleysides, a London based design firm, has designed Levi's stores literally around the world and though they are very familiar with the "vernacular," the space in Berlin was a major problem. In a three story space the ground floor level is relatively small (915 sq. ft.) and the mezzanine is even smaller (375 sq. ft.) and the main selling space is the uppermost level with 3,280 sq. ft. Jeff Kindleysides, Director of Design of the design firm said, "It's in a very prominent position within the retailing area of Berlin. It's a challenging design inasmuch as the major activity takes place on the first floor—two levels up—and above the mezzanine. Visually, it's a huge opportunity to unify the floors with the total Levi's presence and make the whole thing one big statement."

Some of the floors were actually cut away and thus the space was opened up so that a shopper could visually appreciate the volume of the entire store. To lead the shoppers up to the top selling area, "We created huge graphics going through the floors to create a draw and get customers to appreciate from a distance that there is more than one floor. We wanted to get them thinking—'I want to go in and investigate that.'"

The designers used the Levi's signature blue color to stake their claim on the space. The arched windows of the building facade were covered with blue film as well as the glass inside the elevator shaft. Blue lighting was used in several areas to reinforce the message. The entry level is used almost as a display window and shoppers get a "sampling" of the range of product contained above. An opening cut in the ceiling—near the window wall—leads the shopper's eye to the levels above where things are really happening. A brilliant red wall—easily seen

DESIGNER: **Checkland Kindleysides,** London

from the street—makes a dynamic statement here and it extends up almost 35 ft. to the uppermost level of Levi's. A structural metal column, in front of the feature wall, not only contains the lighting equipment that enhances the wall but speakers which are part of the store's audio system. Another element that reinforces the upward movement through the space is the elevator shaft with the aforementioned blue tinted glass which has been further intensified by the lighting. Steel framed partitions, on ground level, hold blue tinted glass and a bluish colored slate pavement is laid on the floor. Chrome yellow curtains surround a circular bar that extends off the red wall and converts to an on-the-floor dressing room when needed. Levi graphics are superimposed on the walls and set the scene for the merchandise while the

HVAC system and electrical conduits snake around just under the white washed ceiling.

The mezzanine carries a display of vintage denims on panels while audio/visual projections show lifestyle images on two screens and thus make this stopover point part of the Levi Experience. A "gate" system for showing and storing product was developed for the main selling level— the top level—of this store. The "gates" are like doors in front of a closet—and they can be opened, closed or angled to reveal what is stocked behind it. The face of this panel system incorporates sockets into which a variety of attachments can be set so that merchandise, accessories and graphics can be added or changed as required. In addition, merchandise is also shown on freestanding floor fixtures. To light the

store the designers used metal halide floods and projectors as well as some halogen spotlights. All the existing fixtures were relamped with Philips Mastercolor ceramic metal halide lamps to ensure excellent color rendition and a warm white ambiance.

Throughout there is a club-like feeling to the Levi's store in Berlin with a DJ area, theatrical lighting, audio/visual projections, CD listening booths and even Internet access stations—and the pervading blue light. The store manager for Levi Strauss Europe, Middle East and Asia, Henry Barnes, said, "The store is pure Rock 'n' Roll. It offers the consumer a stimulating, entertaining, and cool environment for the ultimate shopping experience. Bright colors, music-inspired visuals and contemporary graphics combine to create an electric atmosphere."

DECKER SPORTS

Mason City, IA

DESIGNERS:
WD Partners Retail Design Group, Columbus, OH
DESIGN TEAM:
PRINCIPAL IN CHARGE: **Peter Macrae**
SENIOR DESIGNER: **LuAnn Carlton**
DESIGNER: **Kristen Labida**
GRAPHIC DESIGNER: **Christopher Michaels**

ARCHITECT: **Bergland & Cram Architects,** Mason City, IA
PHOTOGRAPHY: **Courtesy of WD Partners**

Anybody in the know about purchasing sporting goods for schools, colleges and neighborhood leagues in the state of Iowa already know about Decker Sports. When Decker Sports decided to expand their merchandise offering to the public, they invited WD Partners of Columbus and their Retail Design Group to create the brand identity and retail environment for the company in its new 22,000 sq. ft. home.

WD "leveraged the company's heritage of service to scholastic and neighborhood athletic programs by incorporating elements of small town Americana into the interior focal displays as well as the store's exterior." At night, the store's signature colors of red, white and blue make a strong statement. The bold logo incorporates the look of basketball netting and also announces the brand from the street. Shoppers are invited to step through the high, wide and handsome expanse of glass surrounding the entrances into the store. The "prow" of the building

is a one and a half story curtain wall that acts as a display window. The external steel frame extends above the roofline with its brightly colored flying pennants. Inside, the open metal ceiling floats high above the variety of flooring materials used below. A bright red drive aisle leads the shopper through the space. Changing displays add a sense of excitement as do the products with the logos of the local colleges and league teams which are shown on a black slat grid against a light colored wall.

The shoe department, which provides the highest sales volume, occupies the most prominent position within the store. A semi-circle of brightly-colored vertical wall panels present the athletic shoes by brand name. According to Peter Macrae of Retail Design Group, "Wedge-shaped radial display tables and benches front the shoe wall, anchored by a floor-to-ceiling focal display of featured styles."

The cash/wrap is prominently located and for this unit the designers

took as their source of inspiration the "press box" one might find in a local arena or stadium. "The feeling of enclosure starts from the sloping perforated metal soffit above with suspended cobalt blue pendant accent lighting to the black laminate showcases below with base cabinets, flanking vendor showcases and back wrap." The Decker Sports brand logo is firmly reinforced here-before the shopper leaves the store. The shopper, while waiting to pay for selected items, has a variety of impulse purchase options offered here as well.

Bamboo flooring, a chain link fencing canopy as well as real basketball hoops add a sense of "being there" to the basketball and softball areas at the rear of the store. The store's owner, Bob Lemon, is thrilled with the shoppers' reaction to the store. "It reminds them of a big city store, but with the customer service of a local, small-town store."

GLOBETROTTER

Berlin, Germany

"Everything you need for traveling" and the outdoor lifestyle describes the new 45,500 sq. ft. super store designed by Prof. Holger Moths in conjunction with Umdasch Shop Concepts. The Globetrotter flagship store is located in Berlin and it contains over 12,000 different articles representing over 600 brand names including North Face, Tatonka and Ortleib.

According to Margitta Heldt-Krone, head of the retail store, "When we display merchandise, we make a complete job of it." When the shopper steps into the vast expanse of space, he or she is not only impressed by the size of the store and the range of the merchandise but by "the spectacular and perfectly staged thematic settings in the sales area." All the fixtures and fittings that make this operation work so well were provided by Umdasch Shop Concepts of Amstetten. "Extremely variable (flexi-

ble and adaptable) systems were employed, enabling us to experiment with pictures and lattice components. In general, we endeavored to achieve a high degree of flexibility with respect to the shop fittings," said Wieger Krul, Umdasch's project manager.

In addition to the fittings there is a 42$\frac{1}{2}$ ft. long and almost 10 ft. high stone wall and numerous deco pedestals with stylized mannequins that not only set the stage for shopping but add a sense of fun and animation as well. Another unique feature is the artificial boat basin which can be covered over to convert into a stage for fashion shows, special events or promotions. There are also framed vision screens on the floor and a concealed video screen which runs events or slide shows. "All together these elements shape Globetrotter into THE store of the future." Flexibility and functionality—combined with service

and theme elements—are the strong points of this store's design concept. "The outstanding cooperation with the architect and the Globetrotter team enabled an out-of-doors lifestyle temple to be created that is in its own class," said Wieger Krul.

ARCHITECT/DESIGNER: **Prof. Holger Moths**
FIXTURES/FITTINGS: **Umdasch Shop Concept,** Amstetten, Germany
UMDASCH'S PROJECT MANAGER: **Wieger Krul**
PHOTOGRAPHY: **Courtesy of Umdasch**

THE NORTH FACE

Beverly Hills, CA

Who would expect to find The North Face—a premier supplier of innovative and world famous apparel, footwear and equipment for the adventurous "explorers" of the outdoor world—just off upscale and all-dressed-up Rodeo Drive in Beverly Hills? Well, it is there in the 7,500 sq. ft. space and the new prototype design by JGA Inc. shows off "a distinctive retail environment" that will, hopefully, inspire and encourage shoppers to follow The North Face credo—"Never Stop Exploring."

To celebrate the "heritage of outdoor exploration," as the shopper enters there is an original, hand-carved Indonesian wood door and a wall of cascading water. Throughout the store there are authentic and multi-cultural design pieces from regions around the world where the company has sponsored expeditions such as an antique wedding chest from India, classic Chinese doors that once were part of a nobleman's palace and a Spirit House from Thailand. These units are intertwined with modern elements that play up the technological advances in the creation of the product line.

Leaving the natural stone, winding path the visitor is aware of the large, stone-like sculptural arch that spans the width of the store like a giant proscenium in front of the actual selling floor. Contrasting this rough texture is a wall unit inspired by a Japanese Bell and here are exhibited large photographic images of The North Face athletes. This is next to a pole system that holds a display of active footwear. The antique trunks and chests, mentioned previously, are topped with glass units to serve as on-the-floor feature display cases and they mix it up with the machined form of stainless steel columns and rear illumi-

DESIGN: **JGA, Inc.,** Southfield, MI
CHAIRMAN: **Ken Nisch**
CREATIVE DIRECTOR: **Mike Curtis**
PROJECT MANAGER: **Arvin Stephenson**

For The North Face
VP OF RETAIL: **Sandy Wait**
SR. MANAGER STORE DESIGN/VM: **David Curtis**
DIR. OPERATIONS & FINANCE, RETAIL:
James H. Thomson
DIR. OF STORES: **Rich Marini**

PHOTOGRAPHY: **Laszlo Regos
Photography,** Berkley, MI

nated panels of acrylic that add an "icy coolness" to the area.

Furthering the concept of contrasting textures, the floor fixtures and service counters feature sandblasted pine wood accented with stainless steel and hand-polished perimeter merchandising panels. The "vertically overscaled" fitting rooms are surrounded by a curved outer shell of maple wood to "create the feeling of interacting with nature—as one would encounter in a crevasse." Another of the unique features is the footwear testing ramp which is paved with myriad rocks and stones so the walker/climber can actually feel how the shoes grip and hold on the simulated terrain. Stainless steel hand rails for support are attached to the sandblasted pine unit which also has shelves on either side. To complete the look of the store, dark oak timber strips divide the mottle textured, composite concrete floor into a giant grid.

Sandy Wait, VP of Retail for The North Face said, "Our goal in developing this store was to create a new design standard in outdoor retailing through innovative fixtures and displays that will inspire shoppers to explore the outdoors." In achieving the client's objective, JGA, Inc. used "artifacts and architectural details to become key focal elements perceptually" and thus "establish the unique brand positioning." An eclectic but subtle contrast of materials provides the "rough and smooth/hard and soft environment" in which the products will ultimately be used. For the target customers—from the climbers of mountains and global trekkers to the sophisticated urbanites—they will find in this new design the "sense of energy that is consistent with the elemental spirit of The North Face brand."

MCM

Dusseldorf, Germany

DESIGN: **Studio Gruschwitz,** Munich, Germany
FENG SHUI DESIGNER: **Stefan Gruschwitz**
PHOTOGRAPHER: **Foto Studio Suhan,** Dusseldorf, Germany

When one hears "Feng Shui" one somehow thinks of stores in Asia, the Pacific Rim or even the west coast of the U.S. But Feng Shui is also alive and thriving in Dusseldorf, Germany where Studio Gruschwitz of Munich just completed a new retail design for the upscale and elegant MCM product line. This international luxury label opened a 150 sq. m. ground level shop on a high end shopping street and "the harmonic ambiance reflects the new mark consciousness of MCM."

According to Stefan Gruschwitz, "the design of the ground plan was done following the prionciples of Feng Shui. In this Asiatic teaching of harmonious housing and working conditions, it is decisive to lay out the plan in accord with the Eight Goals of Life: family, children, fortune, knowledge, career, helpful people, marriage and fame." With these concepts foremost, the designers selected the materials for the floors and the walls and for the placement of the products and their presentation. A golden wall of falling water not only provides a striking focal element and visual delight, but — according to Feng Shui—gives off energy as well as a feeling of freshness and clarity. "The interplay of modern interior design and the ancient Feng Shui philosophy creates an elegant, harmonious ambiance in an accomplished form." Lacquered furniture and walls painted in Spatoolato Venetiano create the right background for the glamorous and luxury fashion brand. Another spe-

cial Feng Shui accent—in addition to the water wall—is the specially-created palette of aromas and scents that are used to further "harmonic equilibrium" while in the shop.

The floors are tiled with Estremoz Bianco Cristal marble. A circular accent band in the tiled floor leads the shopper to the centrally located, circular counter. The rest of the floor and even the walls are filled with soft curves and arc and sharp, pointed corners are

avoided. The walls are painted a creamy white color in a costly and painstaking technique that requires several successive layers to be applied and the end result shimmers with a variety of subtle color variations. The merchandise is set into recesses in the curved walls and the flat edges around the niches "create an optical frame" that helps to accentuate the enclosed product presentation. The glass shelves that support the smaller pieces are partially

illuminated from above. The on-the-floor fixtures and furniture are lacquered with the same process as the walls to achieve the lustrous creamy white finish and they are topped with the white marble. A floating presentation table/bar has a thick, crystal glass top supported on a stainless steel leg while the consoles and luggage platforms are overlaid with white leather pads. The dramatic column is hand finished with gold leaf.

The aforementioned water wall is accented with an applied MCM logo which stands away from the gold leafed rear wall and the circulating water streams down between the two. The water is collected in a stainless steel trough and underwater spots combine with the CDMT spots in the ceiling as well as the indirect light from the half back illuminated consoles to create "the moving light reflexes on the water wall." The gold leaf is also used on the wood frames that surround the giant mirrors outside the changing rooms.

The interior of the store is illuminated by a combination of CDMT discharge spots (partially scuttled in the lighting troughs used to keep the ceiling "free and clear") and low voltage spots. The recesses are back lit and that also lights up the back walls. A raised circular ring, in the center of the ceiling, makes the lighting here sharper and brighter.

The large fenestration of the shopfront puts the whole white and gold store on display. The shop window features display turntables covered with white leather pads. A hanging bar system floats overhead with a combination of CDMT lamps and single low voltage spots. This new brand image for MCM combines contemporary sophistication and visual presentation with the lifestyle principles of ancient Feng Shui—and the end result is quite stunning.

ACTION LEATHER

Toronto, ON, Canada

DESIGN: **ll X lV Design,** Toronto, ON
PHOTOGRAPHY: **David Whittaker**

Though Action Leather Co. was a great success in their giant operation 40 minutes drive from downtown Toronto, the company knew there was an important new market that they were not reaching. The busy, young, in-town, loft-living urban professionals who wouldn't make the drive. If they did they would find Acton's line of leather outerwear, accessories, gifts and furniture both attractive and desirable. They would prefer to shop in a "more sleek and modern aesthetic." So—if they wouldn't come to the "mountain"— the "mountain" came to them.

To design Acton's new superstore in Toronto's hottest downtown location, ll X lV Design of Toronto was asked to create the new lifestyle look in the 15,000 sq. ft. space. While respecting the historic architecture of the neighborhood, the designers created this exciting, contemporary shopping environment. To make a more impressive statement streetside, the original single door was replaced by a pair of glass and wood doors surmounted by a classically detailed ornamental framework and brushed, channel-lit, metal signage letters.

The space is a combination of two sites: an original 1800s building with an addition two times the size of the original area and the two areas were separated by the original brick exterior walls. A single, sliding steel door was the only connection between the two. That door was replaced by multiple 10 ft. openings and now the fashion collection is located up front and the furniture selection is in the rear. The huge selling floor includes "discrete" areas for men's, women's, fashion accessories, and specialty products as well as furniture and home accessories. "Creating cross promotion opportunities, the designers

positioned furniture pieces within the fashion department and mannequins near the furniture displays, and added central 'runway ramps' to highlight key products from both lines."

Since the leather goods are mostly neutral in color and similar in texture, the designers tried to create "variety and interest" in the high ceilinged space with its fine pine wood floors and the sandblasted original brick walls. Fixtures vary in height and the company's signature red color appears on the logo on some of the drywall partitions as well

as on selected leather rugs and ottomans used throughout the space. Huge printed vinyl mesh scrims, suspended by aircraft cables, add graphic interest and delineate the rear furniture area. In addition, large wall images are used to identify the different selling areas and also to backdrop the cash desks.

Sturdy, brushed chrome tube floor fixtures support the heavy, hanger-hung leather garments while a matching, multi-purpose outrigger system supports shelving or additional hanging at various levels on the walls. In

addition there are chocolate stained MDF and clear maple furniture-style nesting tables and credenzas on the floor. A modular cash/wrap makes it possible to handle the weighty garments while still displaying small and costly accessories and leathercare products. Special fixturing devices were designed for hanging leather hides which shoppers may handle and for the display of hats and handbags. All this is on show under the concealed track lighting which is accented with pendant fixtures. This is a store worth driving to!

LeSPORTSAC

Madison Ave., New York, NY

DESIGN: **S. Russell Groves,** New York, NY
PRINCIPAL IN CHARGE: **S. Russell Groves**
PROJECT MANAGER: **Daniel Wismer**
ARCHITECT: **R. Ceretti + Associates,** New York, NY

For LeSportsac
PRESIDENT & CEO: **Timothy Schifter**
VP OF VM & STORE DESIGN: **Paul Sanchez**
STORE DESIGN PROJECT COORDINATOR: **Waleska Vega**

PHOTOGRAPHY: **Michael Weschler,** Los Angeles, CA

"We wanted to present, in one box, the entire new face of LeSportsac—the product, visual merchandising, advertising and an architectural environment that would speak to the contemporary nature of the brand." Thus spoke Timothy Schifter, President and CEO of LeSportsac. And, to accomplish this look in the 2,400 sq. ft. space on Madison Avenue in New York City, he called upon the talents of S. Russell Groves also of New York.

The crisp white interior with its seamless epoxy resin, clear cerulean blue floor covering was inspired by "the fashionable functionality of the re-envisioned LeSportsac product" which is now targeted at a "young, fashion conscious market." The blue color "speaks to the vitality of the brand." The concept of the fixturing is based on the LeSportsac product which is strong but lightweight. The custom metal elements (the wall shelving, display units, tables) are made from continuous thin sheets of metal which are stamped and bent into various configurations—"transforming the planar, lightweight material into an object of depth and dimension." These are finished with a white powder coat of paint and "played out against the solid table and

base elements in a dark wood veneer."

"These sinuously-curved elements in conjunction with decorative pieces including Saarinen tables and Jacobsen light fixtures, imply an aerodynamic bent—and harken back to the origins of the product." LeSportsac is a product of the '70s when air travel became a more popular and universal thing and there was a need for an inexpensive, durable and collapsible travel bag.

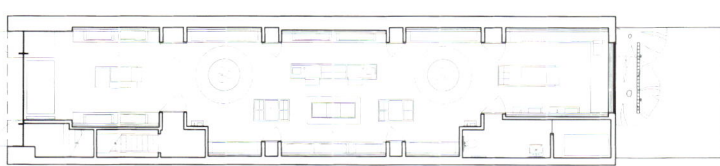

JONES BOOTMAKER

Bromley, UK

Dalziel + Pow were approached by Jones Bootmaker to "create a unique brand identity that conveyed confidence—with a contemporary appeal." The designers thus incorporated a variety of special details "to create a retail experience that ensures a distinct and individual personality." The store, shown here, is located in Bromley and it followed closely behind the prototype store located in Sheffield.

According to the store's designer, "The design conforms to the strong use of lines illustrated through shelving units, furniture and lighting." The graphic "straplines" are used to define areas—delineate menswear from the womenswear—and guide the shopper around the space. The use of "stylized materials" is "designed to be simplistic with strong appeal to a wider audience." The new

design starts with an open shop front facade with a view into the entire space and ends with a large graphic on the far wall—meant to entice the shopper into the space. New graphic images are introduced periodically along with seasonal offerings.

The dark timber floor in the men's area yields to a cocoa colored

DESIGN: **Dalziel + Pow Consultants,** London, UK

Men and shoes, a final statement

ceramic tile floor for the entrance and women's zone. The walls and ceiling are off-white and the "floating" shelves are finished in the same rich colored wood that is used for the cash/wrap corner—just off the men's area. The shoes are displayed on the shelves which carry illumination for the shoes shown on the shelf beneath as well as in glass enclosed cube-like "museum cases" set out on the floor in conjunction with the square black seats for trying on shoes. The utter neutrality of the shop's palette complements the well illuminated shoes and makes the colorful floor-to-ceiling graphic on the rear wall even more of a draw.

Lighting has been fundamental to the design with feature lights used to show the unique character of the store and recessed spotlights to enhance the product display and the graphics.

STOESS JEWELERS

Wiesbaden, Germany

Situated in a late 19th century building in Wiesbaden, Germany, is the two-level, 2,750 sq. ft. Stoess Jewelry store designed by Studio Gruschwitz of Munich. The designers made effective use of the 20-ft.-plus high space which was richly ornamented with stucco work and opened the space up to allow full viewing from the street. The extra high ceiling also allowed the designers to create a mezzanine level for special customer consultations and presentations along with a look into the goldsmith's workshop on the street level.

The shopper steps from the foyer which is covered with ivory-brown granite tiles onto a high quality, warm gray carpet. A polished granite frieze surrounds the carpet. For the furniture and the fixtures, the designers used a combination of pear tree wood with inserts of "root-wood quadratie ornaments," matte finished steel and

ground glass. The glass doors of the display cases are fitted with hidden metal strips, flat fitting locks and special lifting devices.

Along the window wall there is a series of granite-faced panels and each carries three small display cases at eye level which are self illuminated with fiber optic spots. Panels of partially

DESIGN: **Studio Gruschwitz,** Munich, Germany
PHOTOGRAPHY: **Foto Studio Boersch**

frosted glass serve as security wings to either side of the granite plinths. A sweeping counter curves along one side of the main level and it is balanced on the opposite side by the handsome tables and chairs. The elegant leather-covered chairs, in a rich russet color, add "an Italianate flair to the ambiance." A large wall mural by Christian Wahl pays homage to Claude Monet with a pastel, shimmering, water-like rendition which "gives the whole shop a particular charm." The gentle colors of this mural in the receiving foyer lead to the staircase and the consulting rooms upstairs.

In keeping with the Feng Shui philosophy that "water serves as a sign of harmony and prosperity," Gruschwitz designed a unique fountain topped with a glass pyramid display case on top. The fountain stands in front of the "watery" mural and further creates the illusion of "a real dance on the

FREYJA COLLECTION

Windsor, ON, Canada

DESIGN: **WATT IDG,** Toronto, ON, Canada
PHOTOGRAPHY: **Richard Johnson, Interior Images,** Toronto, ON, Canada

The Freyja Collection, a 1,513 sq. ft. jewelry and giftware shop, is located in the Tecumseh Mall in Windsor, Ontario, and it has an open facade of natural colored corrugated board, brushed metal, glass, metallic blue and green paint as well as white paint. To one side of the open entrance is a circular display window that is flanked by a random array of cube displays on either side. This attracts the shopper's attention and also introduces the store's design theme: the circle.

Freyja is the Norwegian goddess of love and the design objective for Watts IDG was to "create an integrated brand experience" that alluded to her. The 45-degree angled shop front presented an obstacle to achieving the required linear frontage of showcases. The designers turned this to an advantage by achieving a unique giftware section. "This design is based upon the mystical qualities of the circle." The scheme is a series of circular shapes layered from the planning of the showcases through to the ceilings, walls and architectural elements. "The undulating forms of the space and the subtle communication elements within the showcases were intended to comfort the customers while engaging them in the merchandise and guiding them freely throughout the space." Even the carpet's color and pattern carries through the feeling of the swirling sand patterns at the bottom of the sea while the space's color palette of white, green and blue— often in metallic finishes—also recalls the sea. Stained maple wood, natural colored corrugated board, clear and sand-blasted glass, frosted blue plexiglass, brushed aluminum metal and the metallic cool colors are used for the fixtures/fittings and furniture. Of special interest are the circular wall displayers and the floor-to-ceiling

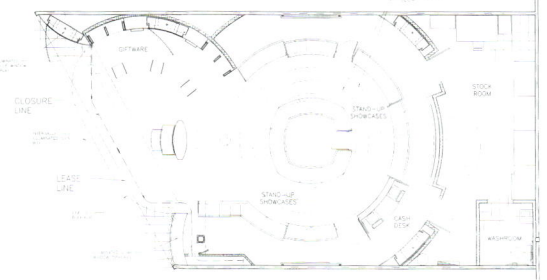

glass display towers introduced at the shop front.

The graphics and signage were developed to reinforce the legend of Freyja in which she flew to Earth sprinkling morning dew and summer sunlight around her. "She wore a necklace that glittered like a constellation of stars in the night sky."

Throughout there is a balance between the ambient and the dramatic highlighting of the merchandise. Special light fixtures combined with the strategic ceiling fixtures add emphasis to the products showcased below. "Surrounding the illuminated features such as wall displays and decorative architectural elements supports the strengths of these light fixtures."

"The architectural display elements were designed to support the refined and unique merchandise that Freyja offers. By combining a selection of unique giftware items with different brands of jewelry, the product mix is reinforced to support each other."

RAFFI JEWELLERS

Oakville, ON, Canada

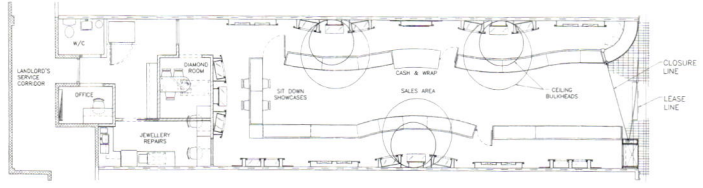

DESIGN: **WATT IDG,** Toronto, ON
PHOTOGRAPHY: **Richard Johnson, Interior Images,** Toronto, ON

This 1,500 sq. ft. multi-award-winning jewelry store is located in a mall in Oakville in Ontario. The designers, Watt IDG of Toronto, were asked "to create a unique jewelry environment that would target and attract customers between the ages of 25 and 50." Raffi—already known for its unique custom jewelry—needed a retail setting that reflected that "uniqueness."

The shopper is invited into the 11 ft. high space through a special floor-to-ceiling curved glass wall. An illuminated sign box with a "new word mark" floats over the entrance. Due to the narrow entry and the elongated depth of the space, the designers "configured straight and arced showcases so that the customers would be continuously intrigued" to explore the store. The ceiling features, combined with the suspended lights, articulate the traffic flow. The wall units with the transparency boxes complement the curved shapes of the jewelry showcases. The free flowing design on the neutral colored carpet tiles further continues the warm, curving patterns.

The walls are finished with a natural rift-cut maple wood, glass, and medium and dark tones of sand paint accented with a blue textured paint. The ceiling is painted a light sand tint while the curved and arced bulkheads are accented with the deeper shades of sand. The fixtures/fittings and furniture are a combination of the same materials and colors: natural rift maple woods, glass, brushed aluminum and the aforementioned palette of neutral colors.

The client requested "a high light level and excellent color rendition" for the store's lighting plan. To accommodate the client's wishes the designers used low voltage lighting in the Bridal section where the diamonds are shown and fluorescent lighting within the cases "to give the merchandise an even wash of light." To make the space seem larger and to create the illusion that the wall units were "floating," fluorescent fixtures were placed behind these wall units. "Special light features also occur and lighting levels and placement were carefully planned to add emphasis to key focal walls."

The designer's statement sums it all up: "a fresh new concept, carried out by simple details, flowing lines and warm finishes what was ordered to successfully position Raffi Jewellers amongst the competitors."

FREDERIC GOODMAN JEWELERS

Willowbrook Mall, Wayne, NJ

What do you do with a space 18 ft. wide by 100 ft. long with half a dozen structural columns creating a number of obstacles in this rather expensive retail space? It took the combined talents of the designers at Grid III International of New York and the store owner Gary Goodman, to turn that 2,300 sq. ft. space in the Willowbrook Mall in Wayne, NJ, into the smart and sophisticated jewelry store shown here.

According to the design firm, "breaking up the space was crucial." They divided the store into three sections "to make it visually interesting" to the customers and added additional columns "to create balance." Designer watches are shown up front followed by the lower ceiling in the central area with its recessed dome over the gold jewelry display. The rear of the store is where the diamonds are

on display and the customer service is located. The showcases are integral to the flow of the design and the space is segmented by the combination of a faceted showcase island and some running showcases and wall cases all made of cherry wood. The island showcases have 24 in. high stainless steel legs which add to the residential feel of the space. The central island—under the dramatic dome shaped opening in the ceiling—serves as "a visual anchor for the store." The custom-designed wall cases are like armoires or etageres and are readily approached and viewed by the shoppers.

Rich cherrywood is introduced on the exterior where the angled corner entrance creates a dynamic point of entry. The wood continues inside on the counters, cases and as frames around the wall display areas. Stainless steel serves to accent the legs,

DESIGN: **Grid III International,** New York, NY
PRINCIPALS: **Keith Kovar & Ruth Mellergaard**
STORE OWNER: **Gary Goodman**
PHOTOGRAPHY: **ZBIG Jedrus**

trim and hardware of the fixtures.

Gary Goodman, the store's owner, was also very involved in the design and in the lighting decisions. "We increased overhead lighting intensity so that it's even brighter. True color is very important when you're selling jewelry." Halogen and fiberoptics were included in the lighting plan along with the fluorescents which illuminate the interiors of the showcases. Said Ruth Mellergaard, a principal at Grid III, "Fluorescent is still the most popular because it is the coolest and has greatly improved but halogen is popular with a number of clients and adds more sparkle."

@ HOME

Cavendish Square Shopping Centre, New Zealand

DESIGN: **The Design Company,** Eiland, New Zealand
PHOTOGRAPHY: **Kelly Walsh Photography**

Targeted specifically at the middle to upper income market, the 5,000 sq. ft. @HOME, at Cavendish Square, carries a full line of hard and soft homeware. The designers of this project, The Design Company, were faced with several challenges including a tight budget and the need to integrate the extensive range of hard and soft merchandise lines in the same environment and—probably most important—create "a home grown identity." In addition, the designers had to make the shoppers feel "@home" while in @HOME and also while reassuring them that this trading company stands for "honesty, quality and affordability."

The finished design makes great use of natural materials to enhance the concept of "an honest environment." There is strong accent on

wood; stained lumber boards and pale maple wood used with galvanized steel. By combining warm and cool finishes, a "warm, domestic personality is achieved that is both comforting and inviting." The "cross utilitarian-industrial" look also allows shoppers to feel more @home. The shoppers are "led" into the store from the mall by the curved floor patterns at the entrance and orientation through the space is achieved through curved overhead gantries (spanning frameworks) "that penetrate overhead space and maintain levels of intimacy." Shoppers are allowed to move freely through the store guided by clear product and category "definition" (signage like "bath," "sleep," "home," chef," etc.). Interest and a sense of theater are created on the walls and on the floor

merchandising units. Special power focal walls feature different colors at different times of the year thus providing variety and novelty. The perimeter wall framework system is "functional and decorative" and is made of an electro plated galvanized material. Support structures divide the wall bays and thus enhance the breaks in the product presentation. Butcher tables with headers are employed on the floor since they are easily adaptable for either visual display or bulk product presentation.

In addition to all of the above, the designers wedged in a cosmopolitan coffee bar, a design center and even an on-line bridal/gift registry.

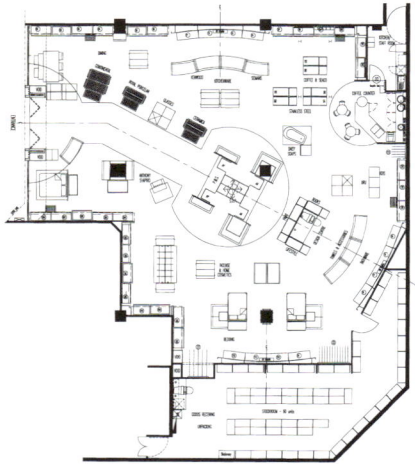

all day coffee @home

pick-up   order

ROSS SIMONS

Streets at Southpoint, Durham, NC

For over half a century Ross Simons has been known as a retailer of world class jewelry, giftware, fine china and crystal. The company's 14 retail and outlet stores represent the assortment of product found in the company's consumer-direct channel but further enhances Ross Simons position of "superior customer value on exceptional merchandise."

It was to further the concept of "the purveyor of affordable luxury" that the designers of JGA, Inc., of Southfield, MI, were called upon to create "a casual but sophisticated environment." As the designers said, "to create a 'do touch' atmosphere and unique merchandising techniques that enhance the perception of choice by adding more innovative presentation and lifestyle displays." It was to bring this new level of sophisticated energy to the consumer experience that this new retail prototype was unveiled in the Streets of Southpoint in Durham, NC.

Partially based on the firm's 50 plus years and its heritage, the designers took their inspiration from the mid-20th century modern design. An innovative layout creates four jewelry loops that are offset and intersected to make the shopping experience more conducive to browsing. Adding to this the space was freed up to include presentation and lifestyle displays in a series of "inspiration centers" which are organized by category, trend, color and/or brand. These "help the customer see both the intrinsic and lifestyle values of the product."

The 21 ft. tall facade is quite unique to its mall setting since it looks as though it was designed for an elegant, urban shopping street. The cantilevered marquee not only supports the illuminated store signage but forms a dramatic entrance way into the store. Added to this is the custom

DESIGN: **JGA, Inc.,** Southfield, MI
CHAIRMAN: **Ken Nisch**
CREATIVE DIRECTOR: **Kathi McWilliams**
PROJECT MANAGER: **George Vojnovski**

for Ross-Simons:
CEO: **Darrell Ross**
DESIGN & CONSTRUCTION MANAGER: **Tracy Zaslow**
PHOTOGRAPHY: **Laszlo Regos Photography,** Berkley, MI

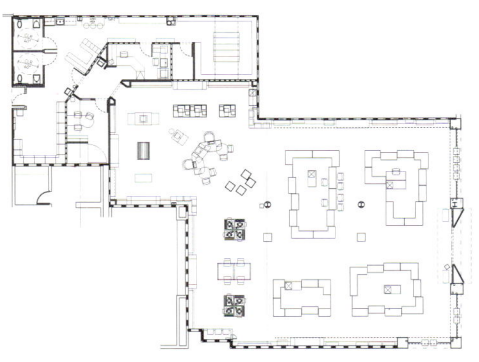

clock with the letters of the store name replacing the numerals. At the storefront, glass cube display boxes rest on cylindrical stainless steel pedestals and "penetrate the glass window to project into the mall through the storefront." That same sense of "geometry" continues inside where the round and square shapes and patterns are used throughout to create a look that is as special as "the original creativity of the merchandise on display."

To create a feeling of warmth and sophistication inside, the designers selected a palette which included a sky blue color accented by the architectural columns covered in aqua and bronze mosaic tiles. These contrast with the crisp, smart black and white striped marble floors. To differentiate the home and giftware department, lower ceilings and carpeting on the floors, with a circular motif, were used—"to provide a more residential feel." In contrast, the jewelry department features overscaled classic-contemporary chandeliers hanging down from the raised ceilings. These are furnished with changeable lampshades that can tie in with seasonal or holiday themes and thus add "a sense

of energy, whimsy and sparkle."

Glowing light elements frame the focal points in each department and the under-lit gray wood jewelry cases seem to float over the black and white floors. Within the circulation areas of the store, unique feature displayers at the jewelry shop intersections showcase product, source or

design stories. These are internally illuminated, oversized, mahogany cubes to display single items or collections and here, too, the background—like the lampshades in the jewelry area—are changeable.

DAMASK

West India Quays, London, UK

Damask is a quality home and lifestyle brand, providing contemporary classics for the home. "The design creates a retail environment that evokes the comfort and atmosphere of an English country home." This new store, located in what was formerly a tobacco warehouse a century and more ago, is on the West India Quays along the Thames in London. The warehouse has been converted into a loft complex with apartments above and retail at ground level. Retaining elements of the original shell such as the beamed timber ceiling, the exposed brickwork and the heavy, weathered oak planked floors, the design concept created by Caulder Moore blends the industrial character of the warehouse with "English country appeal to create a contemporary classic design."

The beams of the ceiling and the rough textured, faded brickwork are teamed up with wrought iron, white washed wood cabinets, evocative merchandise displays and softening fabric drapes. "A simple glass fascia combined with the use of daylight and strong interior cabinet lighting gives the store a great feeling of freshness and openness." A muslin drape over the original window at the rear of the store, which is framed by a free-standing wall, creates a French window effect within the Bathroom section of the store and also enables maximum daylight into the space. More interior illumination comes from the classic chandeliers and the

DESIGN: **Caulder Moore,** London, UK
DESIGNER: **Ian Caulder**
PHOTOGRAPHY: **Courtesy of Caulder Moore**

internally lit cabinetry. All together they produce a warm ambient glow with product focused lighting. "This creates a feeling of natural light and openness within an enclosed complex with architecture that naturally absorbs the light."

Individual areas of the store—such as Bathroom and Bedroom—are delineated by free-standing cabinets and walls combined with fabric drapes and hangings. "The combination of free standing cabinets and individual display areas maximize the merchandising surface area without achieving a cluttered look." Special, custom designed elements such as the cash desk and the lead wrapping found around the feet of the tables and cabi-

nets "enhance the traditional warehouse character."

Ian Caulder, the design principal at Caulder Moore said, "Damask is a unique concept which projects a more personalized atmosphere, which creates a genuine feeling of the domestic, end-use situation. The design managed to project this unique brand personality within an architectural shell which possessed its own unique and dominant personality."

HERSHEY'S

Times Square, New York, NY

DESIGN: **JGA, Inc.,** Southfield, MI
CHAIRMAN: **Ken Nisch**
CREATIVE DIRECTOR: **Gordon Eason**
GRAPHIC DESIGN DIRECTOR: **Brian Eastman**

For Hershey's
GENERAL MANAGER OF HERSHEY'S CHOCOLATE WORLD: **Donald Papson**
ASST. GENERAL MANAGER OF HERSHEY'S CHOCOLATE WORLD: **George Sick, Lael Moynihan**
MANAGER RETAIL OPERATIONS OF HERSHEY'S CHOCOLATE WORLD: **Frank Sheehe**
MANAGER, HERSHEY'S TIMES SQUARE: **Jared Bernatt**

ARCHITECT: **Allen & Killcoyne Architects,** NY
PHOTOGRAPHY: **Laszlo Regos Photography,** Berkley, MI

A great big, colorful—and, oh! so! delicious—holiday treat was opened up and made accessible to the thousands of natives and visitors to New York in time for Christmas. It was the opening of Hershey's Times Square; a 2,500 sq. ft. extravaganza filled and overflowing with holiday cheer and Hershey's branded chocolates, collectibles, apparel, toys and novelties. It was designed by JGA, Inc of Southfield, MI and their design mission was "to infuse the warmth and nostalgia of the Hershey's brand image into the Times Square attitude—creating a retail experience that is an immersive, well organized and fun place to shop."

All the excitement starts out on that busiest of all busy streets! A 215 ft. tall x 60 ft wide store facade is "the largest permanent fixture ever constructed in Times Square." The sign spectacular features 34 dimensional props, four steam machines, 4,000 chasing lights, 30 programmable lights, 56 neon letters, 12 ft. front-lit sign—"plus every major signage technique used today."

That same mad swirl of color, action and lighting takes over inside where the visitor now is surrounded by a whimsical and fanciful chocolate factory complete with smokestacks. "The authentic character of the interior space blends with the technology of the Spectacular (the exterior sign) to represent the brand's unique legacy." A spiraling staircase leads to a catwalk on the mezzanine above "bringing a sense of the store's grand exterior height inside." On the upper levels, 20 ft. high revolving graphic panels display vintage Hershey advertisements "while functionally serving to camouflage stock areas to create an attic space within the store."

Among the exciting brand images

in the store is the spiraling twist of "paper" escaping from the gigantic Hershey's Kiss. It "lends an energy to the space as it rises to the ceiling from the array of sweets and collectibles below." Customers can also create custom messages for their own Hershey Kisses "plumes" (paper twists) or even have their message relayed on the scrolling plume that is part of the Spectacular outside. One of the "smokestacks"—electrified with orange lights and pulsating changing colors—celebrates Reese's Peanut Butter Cups and the collectibles associated with that product. "The Original Hershey's Automatic Gravitational Chocolate Machine" allows customers to see, feel and hear this whimsical part of the "factory" at work while creating their own personal mix of candy at the Fill-A-Bucket. The Company's key brands are presented on a series of varied size cubes on the Wall of Brands. The "high spirited graphic presentation" takes its color and graphic notes from the brands on display.

The clean white background of the store interior creates the desired "candy kitchen" look though the usual nickel and porcelain finishes are here executed on the fixtures in stainless and powder coated stainless steel , aluminum and resins. The limestone flooring is highlighted with unique flooring tiles in areas to reinforce the signature brands. AND—everywhere in the grand and spacious store there is the colorful array of Hershey's packaging, nostalgic advertising art and focal feature elements.

BROOKSTONE

Walt Whitman Mall, Huntington Station, NY

DESIGN: **JGA,Inc.,** Southfield, MI
CHAIRMAN: **Ken Nisch**
CREATIVE DIRECTOR: **Mike Curtis**
DESIGNER: **Peter Garrett**
COLORS & MATERIALS: **Stephanie Bourdon**
PROJECT MNGR.: **Arvin Stephenson**

For Brookstone
PRESIDENT/CEO: **Michael Anthony**
OPER. VP REAL ESTATE: **Robt. Thompson**
DIR. OF CONSTRUCTION: **Martin Nagle**
SR. ART DIRECTOR: **Deborah Burke**
DIR. OF VM: **Scott Swaebe**

PHOTOGRAPHER: **Laszlo Regos,** Bekley, MI

This 3,875 sq. ft. lifestyle store, Brookstone, recently opened in the Walt Whitman Mall in Huntington Station, an outlying suburb of New York City. The Brookstone chain is noted as a popular "stop-touch-try-buy" kind of shop where men, women and even youngsters find "things" of interest: innovative personal items and gifts related to home, office, fitness, garden, travel, auto-or just relaxation. It is a gadgeteers heaven filled with all sorts of "playthings."

This new design by JGA, Inc. of Southfield, MI, was meant to create a meaningful evolution from the proto-type developed six years ago to "a stronger series of in-store shopping zones." The designers also created "an enhanced shopfront impact," all of this to broaden Brookstone's consumer base to attract even more women and younger shoppers. The shop front is now "a wide open exhibition zone" and the front rotunda—finished in rich cherry wood accented with chrome—becomes "a multimedia opportunity, allowing for more flexible reinvention and inclusion of product, demonstrations, graphics or video monitors to be added." Key items are shown flanking the entrance and a saw-tooth wall, on the right, highlights the new products or keys in "see and buy" items of a gift nature. A cube wall unit, on the left, provides flexibility for backlit product displays or environmental graphics.

The layout is "a meandering pattern for discovery" and there are distinct "merchandise habitats." Each is a zone of color or texture anchored by a cherry bentwood canopy through which hanging light fixtures are dropped in the keyhole slots provided. The merchandise is presented in color-brand packaging: red for home and/or office, green for lawn and garden, yellow for travel and auto, etc.

"These zones provide a comfortable setting for interaction, inviting customers to test key products away from the hustle and distraction of the store's main customer aisle." A new addition—for this Brookstone—is Temperpedic "Sleep Shop" which is located at the rear of the store where sleep-related products are brought together and more privacy is provided for testing mattresses and pillows. A maple finished, cube-wall is the focal area for this zone and it allows flexibility in displaying merchandise, marketing messages or benefits and features of the products.

A warm, neutral palette creates "a classic yet contemporary" style for the brand and is accented by the rich cherry wood fixtures and flooring. The wood floors are striped with metal banding and sisal-like carpeting helps to differentiate zones with-

in the store. The metallic and glass signage is similar to the brand name sign out front. The wall fixtures are enhanced by under-lit, polycarbonate shelving trimmed with an aluminum angle edge.

The curved cash/wrap zone "reflects the same industrial character of the store" and it is highlighted by a plasma screen that promotes Brookstone as a "cataloger, internet retailer and physical store." Adjoining the cash/wrap are metal fixtures and a metallic mini-slat back wall offering further merchandise opportunities.

Watch your local mall for more of these new and improved Brookstone stores.

HOTWORX

San Antonio, TX

DESIGN: **WATT IDG,** Toronto, ON, Canada
BRANDING & GRAPHICS: **WATT International**
GRAPHIC PRODUCTION: **Photo Digital Imaging**
ARCHITECT: **Architeriors, Gary Dunlap**
PHOTOGRAPHY: **Richard Johnson, Interior Images,** Toronto, ON, Canada

With Hotworx we introduce the first of showroom design which we hope to include, periodically, into this mix of retail environments.

Hotworx is not only a showroom but it serves as a retail setting. The 10,000 sq. ft. space is located along a strip center/plaza and it is surrounded by office complexes rather than a shopping center. The client wanted a fresh and unique approach to office furniture retailing. Not only did this concept need to be different from the competition but the design had to be adaptable to roll-outs in the future in different spaces and environments. To attract the moving traffic on the road in front, there is an internally illuminated pylon with the HOTWORX logo. The storefront is contemporary with an aluminum metal panel facade and the windows are glazed with reflective film: this is hot and sunny Texas! Thus, visibility inside the store is low. However, 3D individual letters spelling out the company name are mounted over the entry into the store with its 14 ft. ceiling.

"The objective of Hotworx showroom is to work hand-in-hand with their on-line virtual showroom, bringing the customers from their web visit to the actual showroom and educate them about office furniture." To differentiate Hotworx from other contract furniture sellers it was decided to create three pods: The White Room, Sand Box, and Diner Booth. Each pod has a unique function and they are situated in the center of the showroom while the furniture is shown along the perimeter-creating a racetrack circulation. "They get a glimpse of the showroom and yet not the full view until they arrive at the area—thus adding interest and surprise to their experience."

Subtle variations of cream, beige, light gray and off-white are used on

the walls and ceiling to support the bold graphics and the colorful office furniture products. A T-bar ceiling makes it possible to install different environments and also acts as a grid space for the suspended graphic panels. To draw shoppers into the space a garnet red color and a Nevada sky blue are used on the 36 ft. long Chair Wall at the rear of the space. Three full-height sliding panels in front of this wall form part of their "Leap" chair photo. Full-height slid-

ing panels of photographs of big faces reinforces the images and tone set up front in the concierge area. This reception space features three feature walls: The Credo wall explains what Hotworx is while the Embrace wall introduces the brand's attitude. The last wall—1/5/10 wall—explains the delivery model. "The wall mural graphics are bold, dynamic and fun." Acting as dividers between the various displays of furniture are moveable scrims and the

sliding dividers previously mentioned.

Products along the wall—on the floor—are illuminated by track lights while the three pods use recessed mounted spotlights with a dropped ceiling to create a more private or intimate feeling. In the White Room there are also fluorescent light fixtures that can be controlled separately "to provide different lighting scenarios and options for customers." The combination of the design layout, the use of colors, graphic communication and the unique offerings from Hotworx makes the showroom-to-be "cool, fun and dynamic. The store provides all the essential tools for the sales staff to explore solutions and recommendations with their customers."

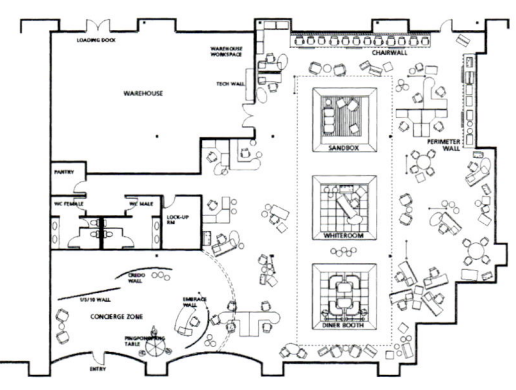

diner booth: 'dye nur buth/ *n.* 1. A place to meet and greet. 2. A nook for light noshing. 3. The perfect place for chatting, rapping, yakking, jabbering, shooting the breeze, chewing the fat and bending an ear or two.

I-MODE

The Hague, The Netherlands

DESIGN: **fca! Retail,** Amsterdam
DESIGN TEAM: **Stephan Pangratz** with **Alexai Drozdov** and **Rene van Rijk**
STRATEGY TEAM: **Ron Cijs** with **Nico de Jong**
PROJECT MANAGER FOR KPN MOBILE: **Ms. Tijntje Louwers**
PHOTOGRAPHY: **Courtesy of fca! Retail**

KPN Mobile is one of the leading mobile phone operators in Europe. KPN asked fca! Retail to create and design a store concept to bring to life the world of I-mode and to enable consumers to experience the world of I-mode. Working closely in association with the client, the designers created this new and exciting showroom/salesroom that was introduced in Japan, Germany and this installation in The Hague.

The virtual world of I-mode had to be transformed to a unique, physical, three-dimensional experience. In an interactive way the I-mode store has become a guide to all

aspects of I-mode. Everything has its own place in the store: services, hardware, content providers and personal applications. The space is divided into three spacial zones. The "Confrontation Zone" is the entrance with the brand icon for I-mode and just beyond is the "Information & Content Zone" which is "the hearth of the store." Here, all information about how to purchase I-mode and its services are centralized. The "Content Forest" consists of 14 curved metal poles of approximately nine feet in length and on these poles the various content providers are displayed and "explain their content virtually and interactively." The red check-out station is a "work of art" in its amorphous and sinuous form of almost 13 ft. in length. At the rear

of the store is the "Experience Zone." There is a huge area with a rounded back wall (36 ft. x 9 ft.) upon which moving images are projected. "This symbolizes the uniqueness of I-mode: with I-mode you have the world in your back pocket." Shoppers are invited to sit on the bright, colorful plastic "sitting rocks" and activate a pop-up screen to build their own I-mode sites. "This is where the world of I-mode enters the store larger than life."

The I-mode hand sets are on display in a sound square of two purple walls which contain over 100 spheres in which the hand sets are visible. By touching some of these spheres, the visitor activates new and trendy ring tones. On the green tinted lucite panels—the "Grasslands"—the assorted accessories are shown on

green pegs that extend through openings in the panels.

According to Stephan Pangratz, creative director of fca! Retail, "Fluid forms and organic shapes, combined with bright primary colors are the main style elements of the shop. This design was inspired by nature, for example the 'Content Forest,' 'sitting rocks,' 'large tulips' and 'grassfields.' The translation of these metaphors into store design results in a futuristic look and enhances the theme of the shop: virtuality becomes reality."

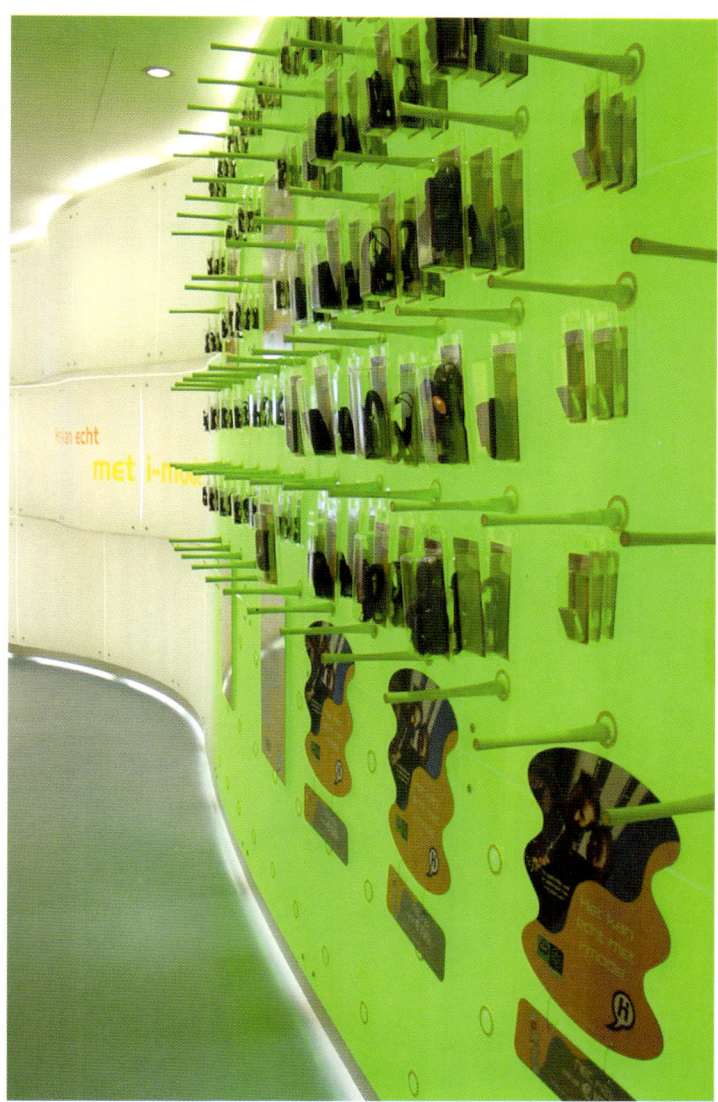

VODAFONE

Watford, UK

DESIGN: **Checkland Kindleysides,**
London, UK
PHOTOGRAPHS: **Courtesy of
Checkland Kindleysides**

"There is much more to mobile phones than just making voice calls or sending texts, and we need to take more care showing our customers what they can do," said Richard Daly, Vodafone's Store Sales Director. "So, we have taken a fresh approach and everything here is geared towards showing and explaining the other services to customers, Finally, we put a live, charged phone in your hand so that you literally 'walk out talking.'" For the concept store that will show off the many facets of Vodafone, Checkland Kindleysides of London was called upon to create a stimulating and inviting environment in which to communicate the features and services to Vodafone customers.

Since the design is a prototype, it needed flexibility and the ability to adapt to different locations and spacial configurations. It had to be "future proof"—be able to change as products, product lines, technology, services and the market itself changes. In addition, the store had to embrace Vodafone's brand values (joie de vivre, empathy, can-do, dependability and innovation) and encourage shoppers to return. Within the flexible store environment a customer can experience a live interaction with any of the many emerging services and can actually work with live handsets. There are automatic "top up" kiosks and unique touch screens to provide information and there is also a facility for on-line ordering from an industry range of over 500 products. For one-on-one action or interaction with a real person there are three multi-function demonstration counters, a business area and even an on-site repair shop.

Vodafone's red, white and blue color scheme makes for a bright, lively and fun setting for the undulating, formed cabinets that seem to snake over the cool white flooring. The bright red walls carry not only giant, color-filled graphics but plasma screen monitors. The store's entrance is part of an ellipse and it

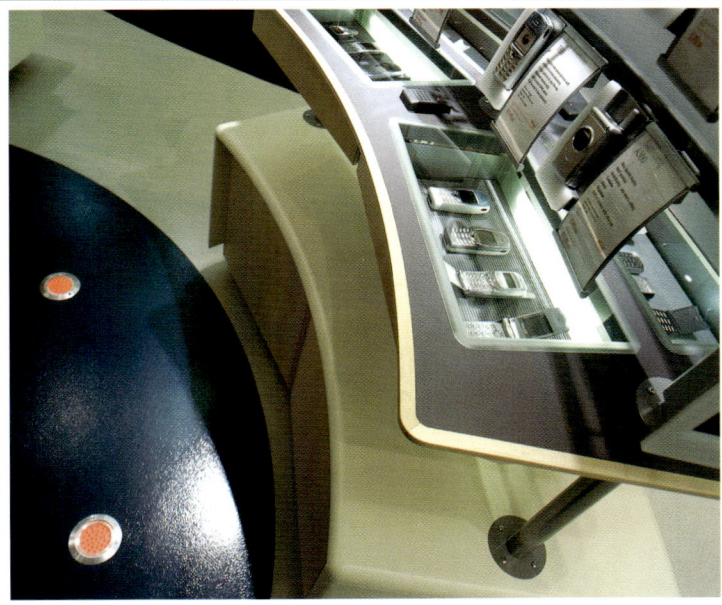

takes its cue from the Vodafone speech mark symbol. "It is presented as a dynamic shape expressing sound, movement and modernity." This feature shape is repeated within the store in the glass panel arch that serves as a divider. "Throughout the store, a hierarchy of graphic images are set as a series of overlays in varying color saturation and scale to provide in-store navigation, depict the services available, connect the customers with the brand values and provide a backdrop to the demonstration areas around the store." Up front there is a faster pace and the latest innovative products are displayed. Customers can download ring tones and such at the automatic kiosks. The central area consists of a hub that acts as a main focal point and where handsets are displayed on curved merchandising units in a cir-

cular format as well as on the perimeter walls where the plasma screens display current services and product features.

The glass wall, previously mentioned, divides the central area from the rear of the shop and it can serve to accommodate back projection imagery. This is the "business" part of the operation. Two glass showcases house the latest equipment of concept handsets and personal organizers. The subtle change of color at the rear of the store and the softer flooring create a more relaxed ambiance where the high value products are displayed to appeal to the small business user. The space shown here is in Watford and is 1,500 sq. ft. in size.

ST. LOUIS ART MUSEUM GIFT SHOP

Forest Park, St. Louis, MO

Way back in 1904 during the St. Louis World's Fair, this beautiful Beaux Arts style building was erected to serve as The Palace of Fine Arts. Today, this is the Sculpture Hall of the St. Louis Art Museum in the Forest Park area of St. Louis, MO. The 600 sq. ft. satellite of the museum's full gift shop was designed by Charles Sparks + Co. of Westchester, IL. to serve "as the heart of the museum complex" and it has been integrated into the original architecture of the space.

There were some big challenges for the designers in creating this very small retail shop. First and foremost was how to integrate "commercial activity" into the Neo-Classical space and provide the extreme versatility required for changing merchandise so that it ties in with the changing exhibits. Other considerations included the secure closure of the shop after hours when the hall might be used for special events and how to combine the retail activity without com-

promising the integrity and essential aesthetic mission of the museum.

A formal axial symmetry was used in the space that echoes the axial symmetry of the hall and its formal niches and vaults. An ovoid planform was adapted for the selected niche to repeat "the soft forms of the vaults" but more importantly—to increase the usable square footage without interfering with the adjacent neutral piers that define the niches. The monochromatic color scheme included using the same paint system of the sculpture hall and matching the lacquers and laminates to it. All the original marble flooring, borders and details were retained and the new hardware in the shop matches the oiled antique bronze hardware of the hall itself.

The interior of this oval plan is segmented into 4 ft. x 2 ft. "cabinets" with totally

interchangeable and relocatable merchandising components. An upper "visual area"—six feet off the ground—is used to "story-tell" the unique product offerings that are inspired by the special exhibit then on display in the hall. Each of these vertical units is self illuminated so that the above-reach showcases are highlighted.

DESIGN: **Charles Sparks + Co.,** Westchester, IL

Project Design Team

PRESIDENT & CEO: **Charles Sparks**

VP AND ACCOUNT MANAGER, ARCHITECT: **Stan Weisbrod**

DIRECTOR OF RESOURCE STUDIO: **Fred Wiedenbeck**

PROJECT DOCUMENT COORDINATOR: **Eric Ostrowski**

Retailer's Project Team

DIRECTOR: **Brent Benjamin**

ASSISTANT DIRECTOR: **Rick Simoncelli**

DIRECTOR OF SALES: **Rita Wells**

PHOTOGRAPHY: **Charlie Meyer,** Chicago, IL

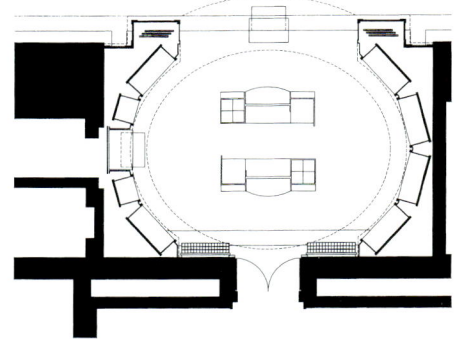

CHICAGO ARCHITECTURAL FOUNDATION

Shop & Tour Center, Chicago, IL

DESIGN: **VOA Associates,** Chicago IL
Re-Design team
PRINCIPAL IN CHARGE: **Nick Luzietti, IIDA,AIA**
SR. DESIGN & PLANNING CONSULTANT: **Vic Vickery, FAIA**
PROJECT MANAGER: **Beth Davis**
PROJECT ARCHITECT: **Steven Citari**
PROJECT DESIGNER: **Rika Semba**
DESIGNER: **Paul Sim**

PHOTOGRAPHY: **Christopher Barrett & Mario Lorenzetti, Hedrich Blessing Photography,** Chicago, IL

Not only did the re-design of the storefront of the Book Shop and Tour Center of the Chicago Architectural Foundation have to reflect "Chicago's rich historical history, embracing its progressive and classical elements," it also had to comfortably coexist in the Santa Fe Railway Exchange Building of 1904 designed by the noted modern architect Daniel Burnham. While Burnham's atrium and exterior design frame the store, the curvilinear modernist glass structure that encloses this area is more in keeping with the International style of Mies Van der Rohe. This element of design is based on the Inland Steel Building's facade of 1958 and here it encourages visitors to explore the space and circulate through the shop. Nick Luzietti, Principal in charge of design at VOA Associates, said, "A soft arc that takes you from the front door to the back door is done in this type of membrane. The glass and steel guide you through the space and also serve as a way to hang and display things attached to the structure."

For a more futuristic touch there is the central oval element "that brings both light and movement" into the space while camouflaging a fixed duct shaft. 3D images can be projected on the face of this piece to create "an abstract, kinetic experience for the customers." The videos sold in the book store and even tour information can be viewed here. A cash/wrap wraps around part of the oval column. A grid layout of Chicago is represented in patterns on the floor and floating from the ceiling. The case goods that line the perimeter of the space are representative of the Chicago School (early 20th century) of which Daniel Burnham was a member. "We mimicked the terra cotta and stone details that you can see on the interior lobby and they become part of the casegoods or skin of this interior space," said Luzietti.

When the shop and tour center is closed, the store and its displays are still very visible from Michigan Avenue thanks to the dramatic lighting that accentuates the historic elements and the products displayed in the illuminated wall niches.

PEPSI WORLD

Toys 'R' Us, Times Square, New York, NY

DESIGN: **FRCH,** Cincinnati, OH
PRINCIPAL IN CHARGE: **Thomas Horwitz**
DESIGN DIRECTOR: **Kyle Kieper**
SR. DESIGNER/PROJECT MANAGER: **Scott Rink**
DESIGNER: **Michael Chaney**
GRAPHIC DESIGNER: **Jenny Kerr**

For Pepsi Cola
Randy Eyberg : Sr. Marketing Manager
Chad Stubbs : Asst. Manager
Scott Hughes: Nat'l Accounts Sales Mngr.

PHOTOGRAPHY: **Mark Steele Photography,** Col. OH

High above the selling floors of the 110,000 sq. ft. Toys "R" Us flagship store in Times Square is PepsiWorld. This is "a three dimensional Pepsi brand experience" within a complex that is filled with color, lights, and visual excitement just waiting to be experienced. According to the designers of this project, FRCH, who worked with the people at Pepsi Co., "It is all about interacting with the brand from a kid's point of view."

The experience begins with an elevator ride up to the floating observation deck perched 60 ft. off the ground and level with the top of the Ferris wheel that dominates the center of the store and actually extends down below street level. Once inside the 1,850 sq. ft. space the Pepsi Experience takes over with a total immersion and interaction with the brand in an atmosphere where "Pepsi Factory meets high-tech playground." A striking light show is housed in a translucent fabric structure or "punch bowl" that is the focus and anchor for "the world's largest soda fountain" with stations that surround a central core. Each dispensing station includes an LCD monitor that features the latest and most recognizable Pepsi celebrities and the lifestyle trends of the youngsters who fill in under the inverted gauzy dome. The visitors are encouraged to create their own "floats" using the Pepsi sodas and the Breyers Ice Cream and cookies and such available at the Frito Lay vending set-ups that are also located here.

A small stage is set at one side where in addition to the video monitors there are life-size, flat cut-outs of some of the noted personalities who appear in the Pepsi ads and TV commercials such as Brittany Spears, Sammy Sosa and Jeff Gordon. Children—or grown-ups—can have their pictures taken standing next to these figures. This Pepsi Live Station is also used to "introduce one-

of-a-kind project launches by stars in the entertainment and sports fields. Standing out under some strong, industrial-style halide pendant lamps is the unique "pay podium" or cash/wrap which rather subtly informs visitors that it costs to participate. "The Pepsi-matic industrial aesthetic" of this unit and the space in general was modeled from factory elements such as the red and silver pipes, ducts, valves and vents that add top the high-tech, and fun feeling of

PepsiWorld. Since the area was designed to be youth friendly, the counter/tables have lower level counters just right for the smaller children. Here shorter stools are provided but throughout the Pepsi bottle cap design of the stool seats is maintained. The checkerboard floor is finished in two shades of Pepsi's signature blue as is most of the surrounding space. All the materials that were used are easy to maintain and selected to resist wear and tear from the countless visitors that swarm through the space. The laminate on the cash/wrap is a confetti pattern of red, blue and yellow on a white field and the same bright, sharp primary yellow color appears on the dividers and railings in the blue ambiance as well as on the ductwork and HVAC systems running across the open ceil-

ing. The light show from the "dome" over the soda fountain also washes strong colors over the ceiling area. "All the materials are shiny and reflective—a reference to the fizz and carbonation—and capture some of the energy of Pepsi." On the wall, outside of this enclosure, and readily seen from almost anywhere in the multi-level Toys "R" Us store is the dimensional PepsiSphere—"A recognizable beacon worldwide." It announces the presence of Pepsi high up above the selling floors.

According to the designers, "It is all about being current, moving forward and staying on the cutting edge." As I see it—it is all about selling and promoting the brand and doing it with style and a smile and not letting the target market know that it is actually being bombarded with a message. It is all about sophisticated "Brand-washing"!

SHOP EDS

EDS Center Building, Plano, TX

DESIGN: **Michael Malone Architects,** Dallas, TX
PRINCIPAL IN CHARGE OF DESIGN: **Michael Malone, AIA**
PROJECT ARCHITECT: **Talmidge Smith**

For EDS
VP & DIRECTOR OF EDS GLOBAL MARKETING: **Gail Rigler**
DIRECTOR EDS EXPERIENCE: **Mary Frances Hoover**
DIRECTOR OF EDS EVENTS: **Diann D. White**

PHOTOGRAPHY: **Jud Haggard Photography,** Bellaire, TX

EDS (Electronic Data Systems) is headquartered in Plano, TX and the company developed a program of casual apparel for the employees to wear at company outings and events —as well as for office use. The company decided that in addition to making these branded outfits available online they would like to have a place—on site—that could be readily accessed by the employees of EDS and visitors as well. The area that was selected was in the lobby, in a nine story atrium, and the shop had "to fit into this environment seamlessly and also enhance the lobby space." This challenging design was offered to Michael Malone Architects of Dallas and what evolved is shown here.

Among the other challenges the architects/designers faced was that since this is an open space there is no electrical or HVAC infrastructure and

the nearest ceiling height was 125 ft. off the ground. Since the building is also open 24 hours a day, the space needed to be secured at night. In addition there was a need for two dressing rooms, electrical service to the cash/wrap and the product displays and the designers had to provide a graphic image of EDS that would be visible inside and outside of the store.

The solution was to build a glass box in the atrium which is visible on all sides and from the overlooking balconies. The HVAC systems and the dressing rooms are at the rear of the store where a solid wall was constructed. Four fixture towers, anchored to the floor, support a steel frame trellis that holds track lighting and is a raceway for other electrical service. The four trellis columns were then wrapped with millwork fixtures that "gave them visual mass and became

slatwall displays for small items and the backdrop for the flat panel monitors that displayed EDS commercials and the EDS website." Free-standing fixture modules, on casters, ring the glass perimeter and they can be moved to reorganize the store as needed and the inner sides are faced with display areas for folded and hung merchandise.

Changeable graphic panels can be

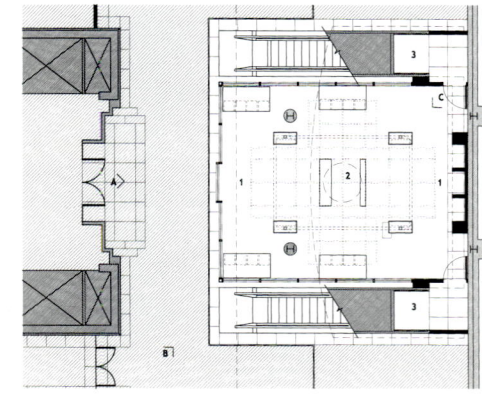

set into the grid that makes up the sides of the glass cube. "The effect is of a large mural, divided into smaller units by the visible grid." Since these graphic panels can be removed and changed, the possibility exists for updating whenever new initiatives are started to bring the store into compliance with new branding concepts. A sliding glass storefront panel provides access into the store and when the store is open the panel slides behind one of the glass walls. The successful end result blends beautifully with its setting since the materials are "sympathetic to the rest of the space—but used in a lighter, more open way." "It has a presence of its own and is readily recognized as a retail store. The concept and execution of this free-standing store within a larger space can easily be adapted for permanent exhibits or even trade show exhibit spaces.

BROOKS BROTHERS

In keeping with the Brooks Brothers new, more contemporary image and with the idea of attracting a younger clientele, the new store on Fifth Avenue in New York City has a more open, lighter and brighter look.

When the store decided to add the new digital tailoring department on the third floor they wanted a quick, easy and—if necessary—movable shop concept. With digital tailoring a customer can be scanned to render a 3D image from which a variety of measurements can be obtained. From these measurements a "perfectly customized suit" can be produced for the specific customer. The solu-

tion called for a high-tech procedure, a high tech setting and a high tech system to make it all possible. Using systems designed by ALU of New York, the results are shown here.

The elements of the system were combined to create the striking circular focal pod on the floor that introduces the digital tailoring concept as well as an exhibit arrangement of information panels. Self standing floor-to-ceiling, on-the-floor merchandising units were also made of the ALU components that combine hanging below with message panels above.

BROOKS BROTHERS, Fifth Ave., New York, NY
STORE PLANNING DIRECTOR: **Tom Doherty**
VISUAL DIRECTOR: **Paul Sadowski**
VISUAL MANAGER: **Don Wade**
Fitting Systems by ALU, New York, NY

FIDO KIOSK

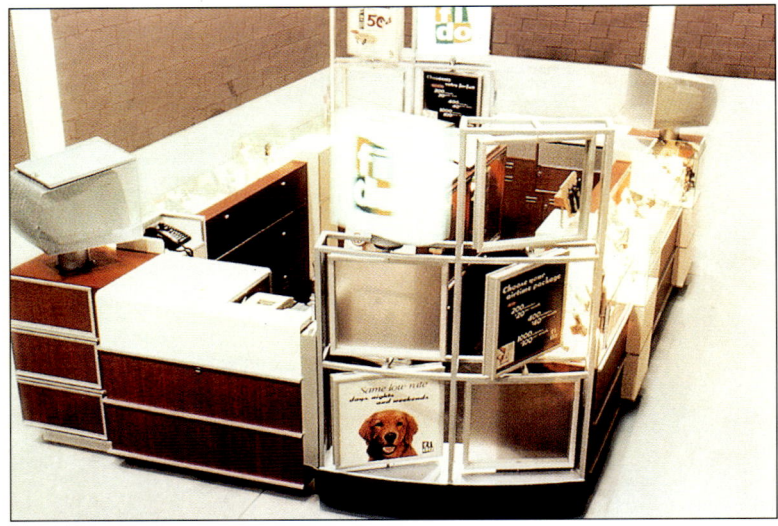

With kiosks becoming more and more a very visible part of the retail scene, we highlight the Fido kiosk which was designed by Gervais Harding & Associates of Montreal. Designed for Microsell Solutions, these adaptable and rearrangable kiosks appeared in malls and other public meeting spaces throughout Ontario and Quebec and they resulted in impressive increases in brand awareness and sales for the displayed products.

The concept is based on a series of coordinated modules that can be combined in a variety of ways depending upon the allocated space or the configuration of the space. In a kiosk design every inch of space is used if not for show and sell then for storage or for telling the message. This design is a blend of industrial and residential elements to resonate with the Fido market of youthful, techno-savvy consumers—and yet it is not meant to be the least bit put-off for the less technical shopper. Promoting brand image and ease of getting across the changing POP messages were also integrated into the design. The success of these kiosks has led to the opening of retail stores in Ontario and Quebec where the look of the kiosk has been expanded and elaborated upon for a full service store.

DESIGN: **Gervais Harding & Associates,** Montreal, QC, Canada

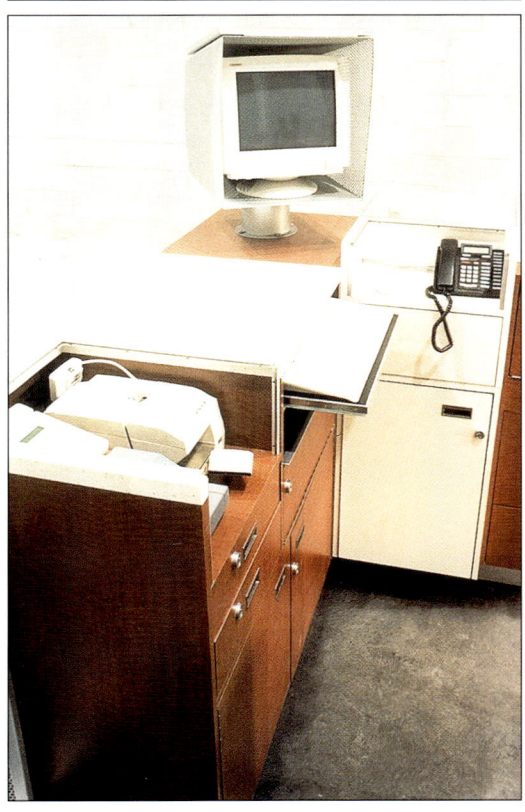

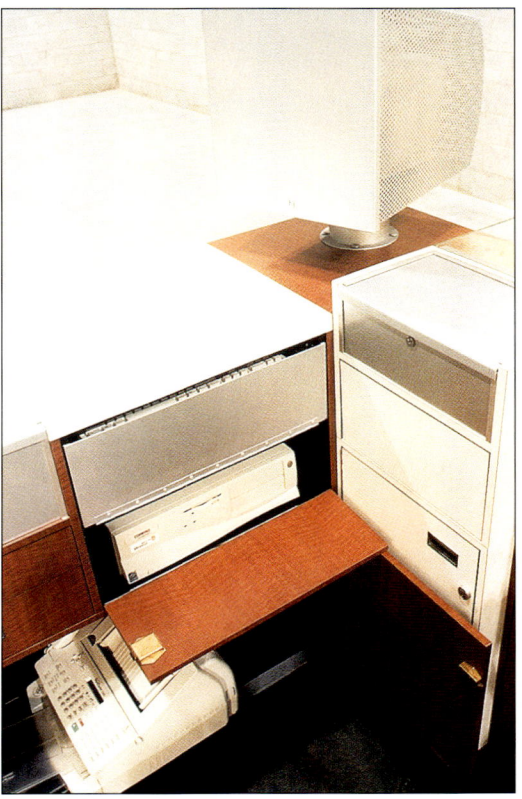

LAURA

Good fixtures can help create good visual merchandising but it takes the eye of the merchandiser to really make it work!

The shop, shown here, is a classic example of what good visual merchandising is all about. The simple but effective floor fixtures are combined with built-in wall niches to provide the wherewithal for the display and stocking of the merchandise. However, it is the arrangement by color and pattern first and foremost that makes the difference. Note how a single garment is featured at the forward end of each of the floor fixtures and how—on the wall systems—shoulder-out display is combined with face-out presentations so that the shopper can "see" the garment before she selects her size and color.

In the wall bays, the upper shelves are set at a uniform height but there is a variety of hanging heights for the skirts and trousers which are hung side out and the jackets which are presented face out. The lower shelves contain the folded blouses or tops that "go with" to complete the outfits. Classic & Classy and great VM!!

LAURA, Markville, ON, Canada
DESIGN: **Burdifiliek,** Toronto, ON, Canada

NINE WEST

The showroom for Nine West is located in midtown New York and to show off their newest available shoes, boots and bags they approached ALU, a noted designer and producer of exciting and adaptable modular fixturing systems.

Shown on these pages is the result of the cooperative venture. Every part of the space functions in a crisp, clean and contemporary manner to showcase the high style product lines. The modular concept works effectively on the perimeter walls where the strong vertical uprights help to add a sense of height to the low ceiling. The semi-dividers, on the floor, not only show-case the shoes but also serves to divide the large space into more intimate parts. One whole wall is patterned off into assorted size rectangles. Colored photographs—back lit—are fitted into this arrangement. Not only are the styles shown in larger than life scale but the photographs add color to the otherwise white space. Interspersed between the colored images are some of the actual shoes—bracket-ed out for dramatic effect. Panels of frosted lucite screen off the windows but allow the daylight to enter. They also add to the clean, sharp look of the design.

NINE WEST, New York, NY
SYSTEMS AND FITTINGS: **ALU,** New York, NY

HERMÈS, Madison Ave., New York, NY
DISPLAY DIRECTOR: **Mark Coats**
CONCEPT DESIGNER: **Lucy Ann Bouwman**
ARTISAN: **Skott Yobaggy**

What would "two weeks in the sun" —or even one week—or even a weekend—be without a beach to luxuriate in?

Hermès brings the beach into the E. 57th Street windows—or the illusion of the beach—with these displays that combine raffia woven boxes with pseudo aquariums set inside and illuminated. Colorful beach towels complement the beach bags featured in the set-up. The background panels are filled with almost regimental repetition of "things" one might find at the beach—or bring to it.

Sony goes down to the beach and into the water in a really big way to show off its collection of electronic devices and computers that some people feel they must take along no matter where they go. Each window has been color-keyed for maximum attention getting and it is the surreal, rather than the real, that keeps the viewer's attention.

In an all-red setting it is the giant sea horses that take over along with the strings of spinning iridescent CDs that become the "air bubbles" in the "red sea." The disks also tie all the windows together. Flying or floating—these yellow sea monsters are big enough to support the laptops and the carry-all music centers as they make their way through the "yellow sea" to bring the Sony products up to the viewers on the street. In a cool blue-green setting it is the mermaid-equipped with multiple new digital cameras—that dominates this undersea setting. The TV screens fill in their own eerie blue light while turtles and other sea creatures crawl around on the aqua floor.

Viewers walking down Madison Avenue are caught up by these strong, monochromatic settings.

SONY, Madison Ave., New York, NY
EXECUTIVE CREATIVE DIRECTOR: **Christine Belich**
VISUAL EVENTS MANAGER: **Leighann Tischler**

SAKS FIFTH AVENUE, New York, NY
VP OF VISUAL MERCHANDISING: **Sal Lenso**
WINDOW DISPLAY DIRECTOR: **Tim Wisgerhof**

When the gloomy gray clouds roll by and the blue sky shows up along with the green grass, the gentle spring-into-summer breezes and the glowing sun—it is time to travel—hit the roads—move on up and out!

Motor bikes, scooters and mopeds are all symbols of speed—of moving—of macho males and dauntless damsels. There is a fun and reckless quality—a carefree and dare to be different feeling to be made with these sleek and shiny vehicles as shown on these pages. Here is how several top fashion stores found expression in these mechanized, motored means of movement.

Elvis would die all over again just to be able to once straddle and move out on the rhinestone studded beau-

ty—all a-shimmer and a-glitter in the blacked out Saks Fifth Ave. window. The targeted spot plays up the sequin encrusted body of the bike and the macho male in the sleeveless shirt behind it.

H&M takes on "the young and the restless" crowd and goes somewhat retro and James Dean-ish with the red, white and blue separates window. The sign up front invites interested shoppers to inquire within for more information on the borrowed moped that makes this simple window a "stopper."

It is time to relax and resort it and the robin's egg blue moped makes it happen. It certainly doesn't hurt to have the stylized palm tree rendered on the bright, sunny yellow back

wall or have the green grass mats on the floor to suggest the setting for the moped and the realistic mannequins in their cruise/resort wear. Note how the blue is picked up in the print and solid outfit and the beach bag on the moped.

The "prizes" are in the window! At Henri Bendel, to kick off a special promotion, some sleek and shiny Vespras were to be given away but before that happened they were introduced into this fetching window. The sketchy interpretation of the pink Austrian shades on the rear wall compliment the mostly black/white and neutral separates worn by the blond-wigged abstracts.

BLOOMINGDALE'S,
Lexington Ave., New York, NY
SR. VP OF VISUAL MERCHANDISING &
STORE DESIGN: **Jack Hruska**
WINDOW DIRECTOR VISUAL
PRESENTATION: **Harry Medina**

HENRI BENDEL, Fifth Ave., New York, NY
VISUAL DIRECTOR: **Gilbert Vanderweide**

H & M Fifth Ave., New York, NY

WHITE

LEFT AND BELOW LEFT
BERGDORF GOODMAN, Fifth Ave., New York, NY
VP OF VISUAL PRESENTATION: **Linda Fargo**
WINDOW DIRECTOR: **David Hoey**

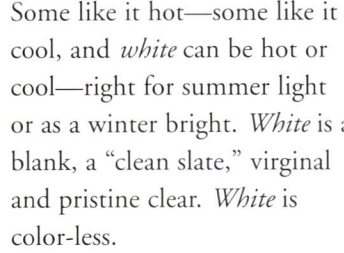

Some like it hot—some like it cool, and *white* can be hot or cool—right for summer light or as a winter bright. *White* is a blank, a "clean slate," virginal and pristine clear. *White* is color-less.

After window displays bursting with color, nothing cleanses the palette—literally and figuratively—as an all white window; a white ambiance as a setting for white garments shown on white mannequins or forms. Primarily, the attraction lies in the subtle play of shadows that add the depth and dimension and sometimes it does take a few small colored objects to make the white seem whiter and lighter and brighter.

Bergdorf Goodman's white abstract is dressed for a party in a Comme des Garcons white gown. To play up the "gala" concept the mannequin holds dozens of inflated pearly white balloons that mushroom up above the figure. It is the expert lighting that brings the dress into prominence. In another window the white abstract is surrounded by thick foam cutouts of the lower 48 states. The state shapes are tumbled throughout the white space to create an unusual setting for the figure. On the floor are some available choices in toiletries and cosmetics that add just enough color to make the white objects seem whiter. Barney's headless forms walk through a mostly white on white window but it is, again, the assorted toiletries and cosmetics—cleverly grouped and amusingly arranged—that add that extra sparkle to the display.

Bloomingdale's—like the Comme des Garcon display—plays purist and sticks with only white in this window. The tennis balls polka dot the back wall and the tennis netting cuts across the display space and separates the players. The white washed tennis rackets help to create a texture-full setting for the men's tennis togs.

BLOOMINGDALE'S, Lexington Ave., New York, NY
SR. VP OF VISUAL MERCHANDISING & STORE DESIGN: **Jack Hruska**
WINDOW DIRECTOR VISUAL PRESENTATION: **Harry Medina**

BARNEYS NEW YORK, Madison Ave., New York, NY
CREATIVE DIRECTOR: **Simon Doonan**
SR. VP OF CREATIVE SERVICES: **David New**

HERMÈS, E. 57th St., New York, NY
DISPLAY DIRECTOR: **Mark Coats**
CONCEPT DESIGNER: **Lucy Ann Bouwman**
ARTISAN: **Skott Yobaggy**

In Hermès' window we have a New York City garden, probably up on a terrace 20, 30 or 40 stories above the noisy city. With each inch of ground carefully nurtured and tended, this garden grows red and orange silk poppies and exotic sea grasses to complement and enhance the Hermès towels so casually displayed on the chair and on the floor inside the terrace.

Saks Fifth Avenue goes all out into the garden to see how the home fashions are growing. A spring green tree grows up in the rear of this dramatically, low-lit setting and the white, yellow, celadon and grass green tableware, giftware and home toiletries are played up to their fullest. Note the watering can suspended by a silk ribbon to make sure that this garden grows nicely for the dress form in the silk dressing gown.

Coach shows off its selection of new spring-right accessories against horizontal bands of strong, bright colors that complement the white merchandise. Green grass grows—like miniature gardens—in small white square pots. They set the time—and the season.

Rectangles of flower-spattered grass is patterned on the PUB's white wall—and on the floor as well. These miniature garden plots introduce a new line of Birkenstock shoes—which are meant for walking down garden paths or on flower covered hills and dales.

MacKenzie Childs is a purveyor of fine foods but they are taking time to enjoy the springtime. They have called in the birds—spread out some bird seed and invited them to share this garden setting with the antique upholstered chair. The blue sky background, the green grass mats below, the birds in flight—who could want more?

COACH, Madison Ave., New York, NY

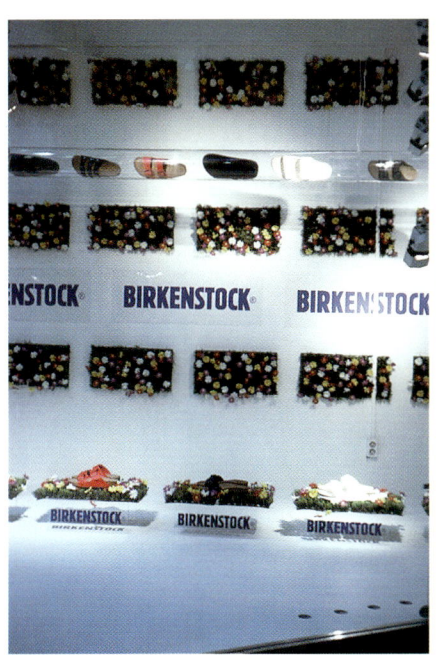

PUB, Stockholm, Sweden

MacKENZIE CHILDS, Madison Ave.,
New York, NY

SAKS FIFTH AVENUE, New York, NY
VP OF VISUAL MERCHANDISING: **Sal Lenso**
WINDOW DISPLAY DIRECTOR: **Tim Wisgerhof**

How many ways can you say Spring has Sprung—or Green-Up Time? In a series of Tiffany-style windows, Lucy Ann Bouwman counts the ways in Birks, Montreal windows.

Fine gold jewelry and watches are the products to be featured and the lighting is targeted at these special pieces. Note how Ms. Bouwman plays the long graceful spears with the more angular and reed-like grasses and then she cuts some down to create a contrast in texture. It is the variety of approaches and composition of the same easily available and inexpensive "props" that does it. In some windows there are golden fruits or even a snail for extra interest. The artistry of technique and the sensitivity to the subtle arrangements were captured on film by Massimo.

BIRKS, Montreal, Quebec, Canada
DESIGN & EXECUTION: **Lucy Ann Bouwman**

It wouldn't be spring—or we wouldn't know it was spring—if we didn't have flower shows to tell us that spring has arrived. Off with the mufflers, the mittens and the heavy coats and off to see the crocuses, daffodils, tulips and lilies—and the hundreds of other flowering plants that fill the windows and ledges of the major department stores.

Macy's has a long established reputation for putting on flower shows with style and panache. This time the windows and the vast main floor were in full bloom with an art theme. Famous painters and paintings provided the inspiration for the window vignettes and for the lavish presentations on the sales floor. Whether it was the bridge at Givergny that inspired Monet's paintings or a Victorian garden that brought forth some elegant Sargeant portraits or a Tahitian setting that Gaugin might have painted—the appropriate flowers and plants where themed to tie-in with the artist and/or the place.

Inside, the heroic scaled gilded picture frames set up in garden plots on the traffic aisle framed living floral portraits. Even the special carpet that was rolled down the main aisle was abloom with art deco flowers.

MACY'S, Herald Square, New York, NY
WINDOW DIRECTOR: **Sam Joseph**
VP OF VISUAL MERCHANDISING: **Mark Minichiello**
SR. EXECUTIVE FOR WINDOWS: **Gil Croy**
PHOTOGRAPHY: **James Mulea**

SHERLE WAGNER, E. 57th St., New York, NY
DESIGNER: **Anne Kong**

Sherle Wagner, the very upscale, up-market and very sophisticated supplier of "hardware" and bath and bed accessories greets the springtime with an outpouring of floral prints on the towels and matching bathroom accessories. The window designer, Anne Kong, created a small flower stand with the baskets (store products) filled with flowers. A stylized canopy is made out of the same fabrics used for the towels and shower curtains. The whole display rests upon a bed of blooming lilies of the valley. The same lilies of the valley floor appears in the complementary window which featured floral designs on elegant bathroom sinks and hardware. The Empire draped back wall, with a sky blue fabric, creates the spring-like out-of-doors ambiance.

Steuben Crystal features its fine cut glass vases which are here filled with spring floral bouquets and placed against a white lattice work background. On the white floor are plants still to be worked on and some of Steuben's elegant crystal animals are scurrying around between the pots and the tools.

Spring has arrived at Trabert & Hoeffer—as the ice and snow of winter give way to the early blooming cro-cuses. A charming and very seasonal call to spring.

Garlands of flowers fall from the ceiling to surround the cut-out figures in the all-white Loren Burr window. The puppet-like kids are wearing some of the new flower splattered print outfits while the floor is a mix of sawdust and dropped flower heads.

TRABERT & HOEFFER, Oak St., Chicago, IL

LOREN BURR
Santa Fe Mall, Mexico City, Mexico

STEUBEN, Fifth Ave., New York, NY
VISUAL DISPLAY DIRECTOR: **Mark Tamayo**

Easter is more than new Easter outfits or Easter hats. In Germany, for example, Easter is a time for trimming the house with bright and colorful symbols of the season. It is sort of like Christmas but instead of red and green for the house—it is yellow, white and a host of pastel tints.

Shown here are windows displays and the interior displays of the Kaufhaus Department Store in Dusseldorf and in Munich. Featured are displays of rabbits, chicks, birds, eggs and flowers—in sunny yellows and the other pastels. The merchandise is effectively clustered to facilitate the shopper's ease in finding what she wants—picking out the pieces and coordinating them with the accessories displayed all around. Ideas for table centerpieces and mantle decor abound as well as gift ideas for those visiting others during the Easter season.

KAUFHAUS, Dusseldorf and Munich, Germany

KAUFHAUS, Munich, Germany

149

Starting with this issue—"RETURN ENGAGEMENT." On these two pages we will feature displays from the past with ideas for the future. Though they have had their two weeks in the light of the display window they live on in these photos and they are now "revived" to be "re-viewed"—and, hopefully— "rethought" for a new life in a different time, in a new place and with different merchandise. Think of this as going to a "museum" where you can study the old masters—for inspiration.

We hope you find these "golden oldies" a new source of inspiration. This month; a backwards look at how Mother's Day and a favored gift of lingerie was promoted in years past.

TOP AND ABOVE
BARNEYS NEW YORK, New York, NY

SAKS FIFTH AVENUE, New York, NY

BERGDORF GOODMAN, New York, NY

MACY'S, New York, NY

LORD & TAYLOR, New York, NY

ST. JOHN'S BOUTIQUE, New York, NY

ESCADA, E. 57th St., New York, NY
DIR. RET. V.M.: **Anthony Battaglia**
DIR. OF V.M.: **Irwin Winkler**

CHRISTIAN DIOR, Fifth Ave., New York, NY

More frames for focus. Escada makes use on an heroic scaled, cut out and hand-drawn, ornate pier mirror to show off the black garments. The curved mylar panel set behind the art-worked frame reflects the white wigged mannequin and the cleverly drawn, cut out and assembled chair and chandelier complete the room setting. Note the cut and curled "shag" paper floor rug.

Christian Dior's display is simplicity personified. The two floating gray rectangular frames serve to highlight the beige handbags and they balance the realistic mannequin in the white and beige leather outfit.

For Tiffany's window, in Munich, the designer used a frame within a frame within a frame as a dramatic build-up to the presentation of a photograph of a ring. There is even a heavy frame around the outer glass —the proscenium—that further serves to start off the voyage inward towards the display.

The molded plastic frames in Ferragamo's display create a decorative pattern on the rear wall. They are slightly off-center to accommodate the two red velvet dress forms on the right who are "wearing" their Ferragamo handbags. The stack of catalogs and the few open and scattered ones on the deep gray floor complete this exquisitely balanced composition.

Frohlich Furs makes a star-like presentation for its matching fur collar and cuffs on the gilded abstract head by framing it with the gold frame. Behind it—in a flurry of fur—is a gilded angel.

FROHLICH FURS, Munich, Germany
DESIGN: **Peter Rank of Deko Rank**

FERRAGAMO, Fifth Ave., New York, NY
VISUAL DISPLAY DIR.: **John Krenek**

TIFFANY & CO., Munich, Germany
DESIGN: **Peter Rank of Deko Rank**

LORD & TAYLOR, New York, NY

WOODWARD & LOTHROP, Washington, DC

From out of the past—Father's Day displays that are too good to forget!!

Except for the Lord & Taylor window which answers the question—"What Father Would Love," the other displays are part of a "Focus on Dad" promotion at Woodward & Lothrop in Washington, DC.

Each window carried a photo of a particular dad and on the front glass his statistics were printed: what he is—what he does—what he likes—etc. Shown in a simple but beautifully balanced arrangement using chairs of assorted kinds that suggested gifts for "that dad" were presented in a variety of levels. A great way to show a lot of product—up front and comfortable for viewing.

WOODWARD & LOTHROP, Washington, DC

MACY'S, Herald Square, New York, NY
VP OF VISUAL DESIGN: **Sam Joseph**
VP OF VISUAL MERCHANDISING: **Mark Minichello**
WINDOW DIRECTOR: **Gil Croy**
PHOTOGRAPHY: **James Mulea**

Think ties—think Father's Day! Even though Dads less often dress up with ties, they are a symbol for that date in June.

Macy's display team came up with these wonderfully fun and unexpected display windows—not necessarily for Father's Day—but they do show how ties can be tied up in a punny and funny way and make the old cliché seem new and different. Nobody was spared!! The catch phrases, in the form of questions, were boldly imprinted on the front windows and what happened behind—with a mix of realistic and abstract mannequins and forms—was the 3-D answer to the question being posed.

"What happens when you get tied into the rat race?" Well, the "rat handlers" are bedecked and begarlanded in ties while holding the oversized "rats" on silk tie leashes.

"What happens when you get tied down to a dead end job?" is answered with the "dead end job" traffic-like signs and the ties used to tie-up the rain coated cast of characters.

"What happens when you get tied down by the office?" brings out the water coolers—or at least the giant purified water bottles—which are now gushing out silk ties.

"What happens when you get tied down to your desk?" shows mannequins bound and strapped down while the back wall is neatly overwhelmed with dozens of memo /reminder message sheets.

"What happens when you get tongue-tied asking for a raise?" The answer is presented against an ordered wall of overblown ten dollar bills and mannequins loaded down—with ties.

"What happens when you get tied down to the bottom of the corporate ladder?"—well, it is when you never get to climb the corporate ladder since you are silk tied to the lowest rungs.

For Father's Day you might try a series of statements that begin with— "Get un-tied from_____"

ABOVE AND ABOVE RIGHT
STEUBEN, Madison Ave., New York, NY
VISUAL DISPLAY DIRECTOR: **Mark Tamayo**

Home fashions and home furnishings are best served when shown where and how and with what they can be best used. Instead of building an entire room—or even a house—to place the decorating and/or practical products, a clever displayperson creates a skeletal setting that suggests the possible final placement of the products.

Steuben's takes its fine crystal and glass objects to even finer heights by setting them in these unusual, eye-attracting vignette settings. The window areas are small but by contrasting the styles of the settings, the displays point up the versatility and the adapt-ability of these home decoratives; from the chic and sophisticated setting exemplified by the smart and stylish modern black furniture to the book filled "study" overwhelmed with piles of books and a big, comfortable chair and ottoman. Again—a few rolls of wallpaper—like the book shelf pattern used here—makes the virtual almost a reality.

Frette, long noted for its fine bed and table linens creates a pair of sumptuous vignettes; one of a dining alcove and the other of a bedroom. Note how few actual pieces of furni-ture—or construction—was used to infuse these settings with the feeling of an upscale, elegant and refined lifestyle.

Sherle Wagner's setting is more fun and fanciful for its line of bedroom products. The red floor and equally red walls set the scene and the bed and table furnish it. The Sherle Wagner linens and decorative home products are set out amid the color-ful, amusing artful send-ups of mod-ern art.

ABOVE AND ABOVE RIGHT
FRETTE, Madison Ave., New York, NY

SHERLE WAGNER, E. 57th St., New York, NY
VISUALS DIRECTOR: **Anne Kong**

MISS JACKSON, Tulsa, OK
CREATIVE DIRECTOR: **Betty Batey**

Soon the long days of summer will give way to the golden glow of Autumn and the green fields and greener leaves on the trees will turn amber, rust and brown. In keeping with the autumnal season here are some fanciful and eye-filling uses of leaves—real or make believe—to create the setting that is full of fall.

Miss Jackson, in Tulsa, looked into the sunset glow in rich, warm earthy colored clothes. What distinguished the otherwise realistic mannequins in the totally blacked out windows were the exuberant and imaginative headdresses of fall foliage. The elegant, vertically posed mannequins seem almost like trees as they sprouted out with the glorious bursts of richly col-

ored oak leaves. In another set of windows the mannequins stand in a shower of falling, oversized and stylized cardboard cut-out leaves that quickly inform the viewer that this is the new look for fall. Again, it is the on-target and beautifully modulated lighting that "warms" the scene and sets it aglow.

Hirshleifer's abstract mannequins are ready to face the first chill of the new season in their sweaters and vests. What season? Can it be anything but fall as evidenced by the profusion of russet and dubonnet colored leaves and the hearty ambiance of amber and red light that heats up the neutral colored back wall.

RIGHT AND FAR RIGHT
MISS JACKSON, Tulsa, OK
CREATIVE DIRECTOR: **Betty Batey**

HIRSHLEIFER'S, Manhasset, NY

SAKS FIFTH AVENUE, New York, NY
VP OF VISUAL MERCHANDISING: **Sal Lenso**
WINDOW DISPLAY DIRECTOR: **Tim Wisgerhof**

Right out of the lumber yard and into the window. Fresh, raw, natural planks of wood, lath strips, or notched and chopped 2 x 2s and 4 x 4s become ideal props for fall fashions. Nothing fancy—no nails—no screws—no dovetailing or detailing. It is the untouched, unvarnished natural material that does it. Illustrated here, Saks Fifth Avenue created an upscale, sophisticated and tailored setting for their men's and women's fashions by hanging 6 in. x 6 in. wood posts from the ceiling to create a repetitive vertical pattern that complements the classic cut of the clothes. A deep purple color is used to enhance and intensify the yellow color of the wood and the camel color of the collected wares.

Macy's used 4 x 4 vertical posts standing in puddles of sawdust combined with 2 x 2 posts of assorted lengths suspended to a variety heights off of the floor. The "twist" here is that the posts have been "roughed up"-notched for a textural quality and unraveled twine tassels make feathery ends to the posts. Note the differences between the two displays. The "haphazard" arrangement, the textural accents and the sawdust to create a more informal and relaxed setting for the outerwear compared to the more restrained and "vertical" composition used for the dress-up clothing. In Macy's display the rich, deep setting-sun, terra cotta color fills the back wall and floor.

LEFT AND ABOVE
MACY'S, Herald Square, New York, NY
WINDOW DIRECTOR: **Sam Joseph**
VP OF VISUAL MERCHANDISING: **Mark Minichiello**
SR. EXECUTIVE FOR WINDOWS: **Gil Croy**

BARNEYS NEW YORK, Madison Ave., New York, NY
CREATIVE DIRECTOR: **Simon Doonan**
SR. VP. OF CREATIVE SERVICES: **David New**
VP. OF CREATIVE SERVICES: **Adamo DiGregerio**

If one picture is worth a thousand words what kind of display story can you tell with 10, 20, 100, or more images—the same image repeated over and over and over again? Ask the creative director and designers at Barneys who have raised repetition of the repeated photo, poster or package to an art form. Shown on these pages are just several of the ways the designers have used the simple, inexpensive, oft-repeated image to either reiterate the name or logo of a designer or brand or the "look" of a top couturier, a product, or even a salute to something like the Girl Scouts of America and their "cookies."

Sometimes the prints are wallpapered in precise vertical and/or horizontal lines to fill the entire background—or floor—or both and sometimes they are staggered like the Armani "eyes" like a brick bond. In other displays they are checkerboarded with breathing spaces of white. It is always something different but always the same till it becomes a recognizable "signature" of a Baney display. All it takes is planning, lots of paper and a Xerox machine—or a nearby Kinkos—that prints black and white and color.

BARNEYS NEW YORK,
Madison Ave., New York, NY
CREATIVE DIRECTOR: **Simon Doonan**
SR. VP. OF CREATIVE SERVICES:
David New
VP. OF CREATIVE SERVICES:
Adamo DiGregerio

MACY'S, Herald Square,
New York, NY
WINDOW DIRECTOR:
Sam Joseph
VP OF VISUAL MERCHANDISING:
Mark Minichiello
SR. EXECUTIVE FOR WINDOWS:
Gil Croy

HENRI BENDEL, Fifth Ave., New York, NY
DISPLAY DIRECTOR: **Gilbert Vanderweide**

Like that series of movies proclaimed, "It is Back to the Future." What was once is once again. It is "deja vu all over again" and "What's old is new." All these old "chestnuts" and cliché expressions are true! Just when you think that the '60s and '70s are long gone and the kind of thing your "hippie" parents were into and wore in their college days are safely hidden away in trunks in the attic, fashion rediscovers them and brings them back as something new. The sleek black motorcycle that revved through "The Wild Ones" with a sleeker, skinnier and shinier Marlon Brando in the '60s reappears as a fashionable prop in Roberto Cavelli's upscale display on Madison Avenue.

Henri Bendel makes no bones about it. It comes right out and says it—or writes it down and announces they are "That '70s Store." The flaming background panel constructed of torn sheets of yellow, orange and red tissue creates a complementary background for the blue denim fashions that never really retreated to the attic or the basement. The cell phone "growing" out of the mannequin's hand is decidedly 21st Century!

Macy's unabashedly went retro and revived the old peace symbol of that period but with a twist. Instead of a circle the "Y" is contained in a red outlined heart. The op-art background, the Marilyn Monroe icon bag, the shredded jeans and the riot of color on the background are all part of the past refreshingly revived for a new generation.

It's "Steel Magnolia" revisited as Moschino's mannequins get permed, bobbed and beehived in a beauty "salon" that recalls the beauty parlors of decades ago. There are the heavy upholstered pieces garishly upholstered in flower print fabric and the hair dryers and blowers that are now kitch antiques. The terry towel turbaned ladies sit about dishing the dirt in today's newest and chicest styles. Ah! For those good old/new days.

ROBERTO CAVELLI, Madison Ave., New York, NY

MOSCHINO, Madison Ave., New York, NY
DISPLAY DIRECTOR: **David Griffin**

UHREN HUBER, Munich, Germany

GODASSE, Munich, Germany

Working with a limited budget in small windows, Peter Rank of Deko Rank in Munich, Germany has often "visited" his collection of the World's Greatest Art & Artists for inspiration as is evident on these pages. He also knows every museum in Germany, France, Italy, England and the U.S.—among others. Whether he is creating a setting for furs at Froehlich Furs or jewelry at Sevigne, watches at Uhren Huber or shoes for Godasse—Rank finds a fine arts tie-in with the Masters.

The geometric panelled background and felt covered shelves that make up the shoe display at Godasse is greatly indebted to the play of rectangular shapes and primary colors that Mondrian favored in the De Stijl period of early 20th century art.

The French painter Magritte—so associated with the black derby-hatted, mysterious figure that seems to float through many of his landscapes—serves as a recognizable salesman for the Sevigne presentation of gold and leather jewelry. The Italian artist Fornasetti, noted for his finely etched black and white classic faces and features becomes a clock master in the black and white Uhren Huber display of watches and time pieces. Turning the Fornasetti face into a clock face was the starting point.

Maybe it is not pure Calder but in the Frohlich window it certainly serves its purpose. The metallic forms on the stabile/mobile in silvery grays complement the patched and "bolted" metallic screen behind the fur-clad mannequin. Even the drapes, on the right, pick up the same neutral color to further play up the rich, dark fur trimmed dress.

DESIGNS: **Peter Rank, Deko Rank,** Munich, Germany

FROHLICH FURS, Munich, Germany

SEVIGNE, Munich, Germany

BARNEYS NEW YORK, New York, NY

HENRI BENDEL, New York, NY

Budgets keep getting smaller and the job of creating window excitement with less money gets bigger. Another new feature that we are introducing this month is two pages of "BUDGET-BEATERS," or "how to get MORE FOR LESS." Whether it means raiding the attic, the cellar, or the long unopened closet or back room for ladders, brooms, mops, cans, and discarded furniture or using up next week's food budget by putting potatoes, fruits, or cans and bottles of nourishment into the display—or borrowing from your neighboring sports, art supply, hardware, toy or luggage stores (or any other source for theme propping)—you can afford to affect great, attention getting windows without depleting the almost invisible budget.

This month we start with PAPER; newspapers, magazines, tissue paper, kraft or wrapping paper—new or used, flat or crumpled, stacked or opened-natural, tinted or colored. What couldn't you do with the Sunday funnies? After using the paper in the window—send it out to be recycled for another time around—in a different form.

PALAIS ROYAL, Houston, TX

VERONA, Boston, MA

ST. JOHN'S BOUTIQUE, New York, NY

HENRI BENDEL, New York, NY

BERGDORF GOODMAN, Fifth Ave., New York, NY

Cheers for chairs! A great prop and almost always an integral part of any vignette setting. A chair can not only support a seated mannequin or serve as an elevation for an accessory display, it can also create a sense of where and when.

From our files of "gone but not forgotten" displays come these old times which have much to say to younger or new designers who must rely on ingenuity and imagination rather than free-flowing budgets for their display inspirations. Old theater seats—sometimes tossed away or offered at auction—can be re-upholstered or covered to turn a small window into a vignette of a deluxe theater or a popcorn littered movie house. A theater program and maybe even a framed theater poster—some red drapery and a scarlet carpet on the floor upscales these same seats which with the addition of popcorn containers and soda cups into a movie where the featured screen offering may tie-in with some fashion promotion. Remember, a credit card for a local movie house will provide you with some of their stale popcorn which still looks great and even the soda cups and straws. Bendel and Bergdorf's windows show the two variations.

Joseph Horne of Pittsburgh knew that Louis XVl chairs speak of elegance and high style and say something about designer salons. While Marshall Field's took a stack of Louis XV chair frames—supplied by a local furniture frame importer—and created a most elegant "jungle gym" for the mannequins in their fancy gowns and bouffant hair styles. The unexpected juxtaposition of the fine frames in such an unusual pile-up backing up the vertically posed mannequins makes a sure shopper stopper.

JOSEPH HORNE, Pittsburgh, PA

MARSHALL FIELD'S, Chicago, IL

BARNEYS NEW YORK,
New York, NY

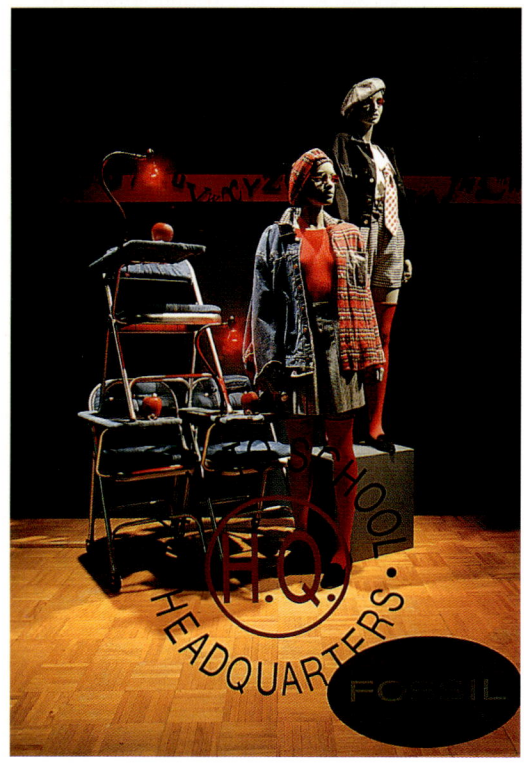

MARSHALL FIELD'S, Chicago, IL

There are endless kinds of folding chairs just folded away and dormant in closets somewhere in the store. Take them out—brush them off—and see what can happen. A tornado can whip through a park and turn the slender French park chairs this way and that way as they did in a Banana Republic window or they can create a soaring chairful experience as they did in Gimbel's corner window. Some of the wooden folding chairs are hung on the wall still folded and others are open to hold seated mannequins. A real spectacle!

When money isn't flowing and desperation is in high gear—look for chairs—any kind of chairs: lounge chairs, Adirondak chairs, wrought iron garden chairs, thrones or even down and out, old broken chairs. Look for the chairs in closets, in unused conference rooms, in cafés or restaurants, the store's auditorium. When all fails, hit the Salvation Army stores or the very run-down second hand shops where cheap and worn out seats are available; then paint them, saw them in half, hang the pieces up or just stack them as Barneys and Jasmine did in their windows.

Also, remember the "beg-borrow and credit" routine. Approach any mass merchant, manufacturer, non-competing outlet store, a neighbor—anybody who might have something you would like to "borrow" for two weeks—"beg" them—"borrow" the prop(s) and then "credit" the supplier with a neat card in the window. You are offering them the window exposure—and a free display.

GIMBEL'S, New York, NY

JASMINE, Boston, MA

BANANA REPUBLIC, New York, NY

BARNEYS NEW YORK, New York, NY